INTRODUCTION

Aircraft exist for one reason—to enable Man to fly. Once an aircraft had managed to take off and lift a man into the air there was a logical and natural progression in the size of machines and the number of people they could carry.

Up until the end of World War I, however, most authorities had regarded aircraft as useful only in the sporting and military roles. Because of the war there was a tremendous incentive for improving the quality and performance of fighting machines, especially after the threat posed by Count Zeppelin's famous airships. The progress achieved during the war years was astonishing, so much so that the pioneer flying machines which were once considered a dangerous eccentricity of rich, adventure-seeking young men had, by 1919, reached an efficient and reliable enough stage in their development to warrant the serious contemplation of air services for the general public.

With a surplus of war equipment and the exit from the services of a large number of trained pilots and technicians, the stage was set for the widespread commercial applications of air travel on an international level. Beginning with wartime bombers converted for use in a civil role, men with a blind faith in the future of air travel laid the foundations of the major world airlines in existence today.

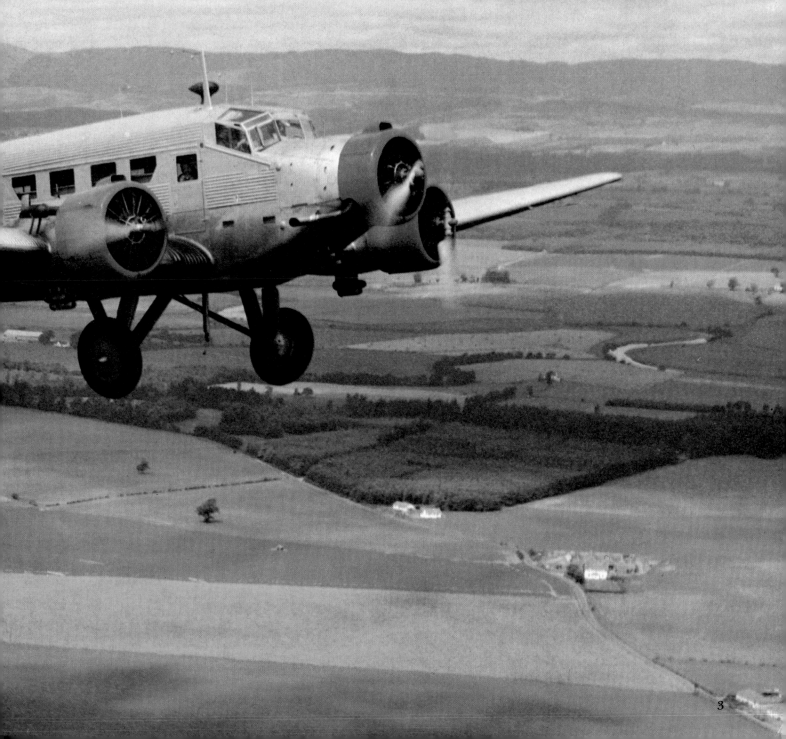

CONTENTS

Blazing the trail

From the earliest stages of man's efforts to fly, the concept of passenger operations has featured prominently, both in works of fiction and in tentative designs for flying machines. Such thoughts were crystallized by the end of the 18th century, as evidenced by the rash of fanciful but nevertheless prophetic 'scares' in British newspapers and periodicals about the prospects of Napoleonic armies crossing the English Channel from France in a gargantuan fleet of balloons. By their very nature, however, free-flight balloons are impossible to steer in the air, and it was to be nearly 100 years before the development of practical airships, with an elongated lifting body, engines and control surfaces.

The thought of commercial operations with passenger-carrying aircraft was never far from the minds of many aviation pioneers, the first 'realistic' example of such an aircraft being William Samuel Henson's Aerial Steam Carriage, the designs for which were published in April 1843. The machine would not have flown, but Henson's Aerial Transit Company failed to raise the capital even to build the machine. Nonetheless, the Aerial Steam Carriage, dubbed Ariel by Henson and his engineer partner John Stringfellow, remains a classic design of its type: it was the world's first design for an aircraft of 'modern' configuration with fixed flying surfaces and propeller propulsion. The main features of the design were: double-surfaced cambered wings based on a structure of spars and shaped ribs; a tricycle undercarriage; a fuselage-mounted engine driving two pusher propellers in the wings; and a fuselage for the passengers, crew and engines, this fuselage forming the structural centre of the advanced concept of wire-braced monoplane wings operating in conjunction with elevators and rudders mounted at the rear of the fuselage. This basic configuration became the norm only after 1908, five years after the Wright brothers' first flight. Power for Henson's dream aircraft was to be provided by a steam engine developing between 25 and 30 hp (18.7 to 22.4 kW), which would have been wholly inadequate to lift the Aerial Steam Carriage, whose span was envisaged as 150 ft (45.72 m).

Croydon Airport in the 1920s

ARMSTRONG WHITWORTH ARGOSY
Type: three-engined medium transport
Powerplant: (Argosy I) three 385 hp Armstrong Siddeley Jaguar III
Accommodation: two crew and 20 passengers

Dimensions: span 90 ft (27.4 m); length 64 ft 6 in (19.6 m)
Weights: empty 12 000 lb (5443 kg); loaded 18 000 lb (8164 kg)
Performance: maximum speed 110 mph (177 km/h); cruising speed 90 mph (144.8 km/h); range 405 miles (651.7 km)

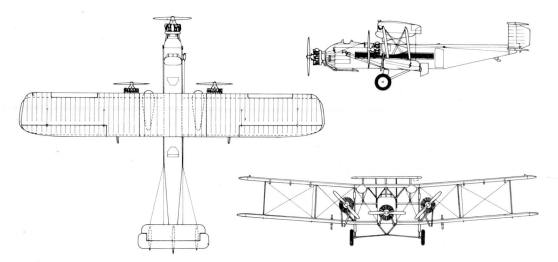

A Handley Page O/400 heavy bomber converted to civil use during pioneer airline flights in 1919-1920

Below: The first air routes in 1919. While Britain was linked to the Continent other air routes connected Berlin to provincial towns in Germany and there was even a route from Toulouse to North Africa

Despite the manifest dangers of combining in a single entity the combustion engine and highly inflammable hydrogen, the dirigible appeared to have many advantages over the fledgling aircraft. Not the least of these were the ability of large airships, lifted by masses of buoyant hydrogen, to carry useful loads, and the relative simplicity of the dirigible's concept compared with the unknowns involved in the design of aircraft. For these reasons, therefore, the dirigible was well-placed to become the world's first true means of inaugurating commercial passenger flights. For this purpose the Deutsche Luftschiffahrt AG (DELAG) was established on 10 November, 1909, with Dr Hugo Eckener, an associate of von Zeppelin, as technical director. The company's early operations were not successful: the LZ7 *Deutschland* first flew on 19 October, 1910 but soon crashed; it was replaced by the LZ8 *Ersatz Deutschland*, which first flew on 30 March, 1911 but was destroyed at its moorings on 16 May, 1911. Finally, though, the company received the LZ10 *Schwaben*, which proved highly successful in a year of service ended by a fire. The LZ10 was joined in 1912 by the LZ11 *Viktoria Luise*, named after the Kaiser's youngest daughter, and later by the LZ13 *Hansa* and LZ17 *Sachsen*. The airships were luxuriously appointed, and could carry up to 20 passengers. Services continued up to the beginning of World War I, and the Zeppelin airships proved themselves excellent vehicles: 1588 flights were made, covering 107 835 miles (173 540 km) in 3176 hours with 34 028 passengers, 10 197 of them fare-paying, in the period from June 1910 to 31 July, 1914. During this period there were no fatalities or even injuries resulting from these flights. Airships returned to commercial operations after World War I, but the growing capabilities of more modern aircraft, combined with the inherent dangers of hydrogen and petrol engines, finally put an end to the type for passenger-carrying purposes in the 1930s.

Moves towards commercial airline operations had already become apparent before World War I. In Russia Igor Sikorsky had embarked in 1912 on the design of a series of giant aircraft. The first, named *Bolshoi Baltiski* (Grand Baltic One), was largely experimental. Spanning 88 ft 7 in (27 m), the *Bolshoi Baltiski* first flew in March 1913

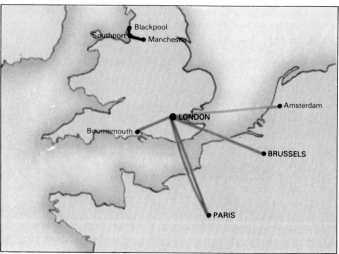

HANDLEY PAGE
AT&T
BAT
AVRO

on the power of two 100-hp (74.6-kW) Argus engines, and immediately proved underpowered. Two more Argus engines, driving pusher propellers, were then added, and when this revised model took to the air on 13 May, 1913 it had the distinction of being the world's first four-engined aircraft. However, Sikorsky had already realized the limitations of the *Bolshoi Baltiski's* design, and produced a much improved, heavier machine which appeared in May 1913. This was the *Russki Vitiaz* (Russian Knight), powered by four tractor Argus engines of 100-hp (74.6-kW) each. Designed as a heavy bomber, the *Russki Vitiaz* first flew on 23 July, 1913, and soon proved basically superior to the *Bolshoi Baltiski*. A crew of seven was carried, and disposable load was 1653 lb (750 kg). The span of the wings was 105 ft (32 m). Sikorsky, however, still had his early masterpiece to come: this was the *Ilya Muromets*, which appeared in 1913 and first flew on 11 December, 1913. Spanning 111 ft 6½ in (34 m) and powered by four tractor Argus engines of 100-hp (74.6-kW) each, the *Ilya Muromets* was designed as an

airliner, with a dining room, pantry, lavatory, cabin lighting and heating – and there was also a railed promenade deck on top of the rear fuselage.

Just as importantly, however, there appeared in the USA during early 1914 the world's first scheduled airline operating heavier-than-air craft. This was P E Fansler's St Petersburg-Tampa Airboat Line, whose service began on 1 January, 1914 when Tony Jannus flew A C Pheil in a Benoist Type XIV flying boat the 18 miles (29 km) from St Petersburg to Tampa in Florida. By the end of January 1914 demand had risen to the extent that a second, larger Benoist flying boat was secured, with Roger Jannus as pilot. Regular scheduled services were achieved with little difficulty, and the operation was soon showing a handsome profit. However, in April 1914 the end of the tourist season and the Mexican war ended the airline operations.

Other pioneering efforts in the commercial field before World War I was the first air freight, a box of Osram electric light bulbs, carried by Horatio Barber in a Valkyrie monoplane from Shoreham to Hove in Sussex on 4 July, 1911; and the first official air mail service, on 18 February, 1911 when Henri Pequet flew some 6500 letters in a Humber biplane from Allahabad to Naini Junction across the Jumna river in India. The first British air mail service operated from 9-26 September 1911 between Hendon and Windsor, and the USA's first air mail service was opened between Nassau Boulevard, New York, and Mineola, Long Island, by Earl L Ovington in a Blériot monoplane on 23 September, 1911.

All these had been in the nature of experiments, however, to test the possibilities of commercial air transport. And just as proof had been achieved, World War I intervened, effectively halting further progress until 1918.

It might have been expected for the Allies, victorious in World War I, to be the restarters of airline services immediately after the end of hostilities. Indeed, George Holt Thomas, owner of the Aircraft Manufacturing Company (Airco) responsible for the classic de Havilland DH2 fighter, DH4 bomber and DH9/9A bomber series during World War I, went so far as to register a company named the Aircraft Transport and Travel Ltd as a subsidiary of Airco on 5 October, 1916. By this means, Holt Thomas

hoped to be able to inaugurate commercial services immediately after the war. However, his attempts to do so were frustrated by the Handley Page Company, which was also eager to break into the air transport business, and by the complications of international law, which had yet to cope with international air transport (though an international air mail service had operated between Vienna and Kiev, capital of the independent Ukraine from 11 March to 11 November, 1918 as part of Germany's eastward expansion).

Such problems did not affect military operations, and soon the English Channel was being crossed regularly by converted wartime bombers carrying government officials and military officers on important business associated with the end of the war and the establishment of the peace negotiations which were to end with the Treaty of Versailles. However, the war had broken the last doubts entertained by many civilians about the safety and practicality of flight, and soon there was considerable demand for the inauguration of services which would allow those moderately well off to move with facility round Europe. But before the British or French could meet this demand, the Germans started the world's first daily scheduled service: Deutsche Luft-Reederei started a service with converted aircraft on the routes from Berlin to Weimar via Leipzig on 5 February, 1919. Only three days later the French entered the market, the Farman company beginning a service between Paris and London with converted examples of its F.60 Goliath bomber. This had been designed towards the end of the war as a two-seat heavy night bomber powered by a pair of 260-hp (194-kW) Salmson radial engines, and its capacious fuselage proved well suited for conversion into a cabin for passengers. Then on 25 August the Aircraft Transport and Travel Company started a daily service between London (Hounslow) and Paris (Le Bourget) with DH16 adaptations of the DH4 bomber, with Handley Page Transport Ltd joining in on the same day with services from London (Cricklewood) using a converted O/400 twin-engined bomber. The difference in the concept between the two airlines was marked: Holt Thomas preferred single-engined aircraft able to carry a small number of passengers at high speed; Frederick

The Handley Page W8, the first
aircraft to be designed as an
airliner. Earlier aircraft had been
converted combat aircraft with
extra seating in place of the bomb
load

**VICKERS FB27 VIMY
COMMERCIAL**

Type: two-engined medium-
range transport
Powerplant: two 360 hp
Rolls-Royce Eagle VIII
Accommodation: two crew and
ten passengers

Dimensions: span 27 ft 2 in (8.2
m); length: 43 ft 6½ in (13.2 m)
Weights: empty 7790 lb (3533
kg); loaded 12 500 lb (5669.8 kg)
Performance: maximum speed
103 mph (165 km/h); cruising
speed 84 mph (135 km/h); range
450 miles (724 km)

Handley Page thought that a better service could be provided by twin-engined aircraft, carrying larger numbers of passengers with greater reliability but at slower speed. The polarity was perhaps inevitable, as Holt Thomas's Airco aircraft were renowned for their speed, and were generally single-engined machines; while Handley Page aircraft of World War I had been multi-engined machines, notable for their strength and great load-carrying capabilities.

With large numbers of ex-military aircraft flooding the emergent civil market, it was inevitable that conversions of these cheap aircraft would get into airline service more readily than custom-designed airliners. Typical of these are the types derived from the main British bomber families of World War I. The DH4A already mentioned was one of the simplest such conversions, developed in 1919 at the request of Mr Bonar Law as what would today be called executive transports: several DH4s powered by 350-hp (261-kW) Rolls-Royce Eagle VIII engines were converted to carry a government minister and his secretary face to face in a small cabin behind the pilot's cockpit. The minister could thus continue to work while in the air. The cabin was of fabric-covered wood construction, the roof and starboard side being arranged to fold upwards to allow the passengers to enter and leave the cabin. Maximum speed was 121 mph (195 km/h). Typical of another adaptation of a wartime Airco type was the DH9C, in which the gunner's cockpit and armament were replaced by a light roof structure to provide accommodation for two or three passengers. Power was provided by the 230-hp (172-kW) Siddeley Puma inline engine, which gave the DH9C a range of 500 miles (805 km) at a cruising speed of 95 mph (153 km/h). Other DH9 conversions and aircraft built for civil use to the same basic type were powered by the 230-hp (172-kW) BHP, 300-hp (224-kW) ADC Nimbus and 450-hp (336-kW) Napier Lion, though the Puma continued to be the most useful engine. These conversions and scratch-built aircraft served a number of purposes other than as airliners, including racing, long-distance flying, aerial survey work, reconnaissance, air mail work

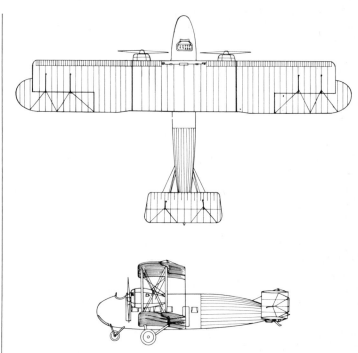

and even aerial refuelling experiments. The DH16 was derived from the DH9 in much the same way as the DH4A had developed from the DH4. But in the case of the DH16, the aircraft was designed specifically for airline use, but using as much of the DH9's structure as was possible to save time and cost. Accommodation was for four passengers in two facing pairs in a cabin in the widened fuselage just behind the pilot's cockpit. Powered by the 450-hp (336-kW) Napier Lion, the DH16 cruised at 100 mph (161 km/h) and had a range of 425 miles (685 km). The DH18 was the first such aircraft designed by Airco specifically as a commercial load carrier, and as such was far cheaper to run per ton-mile than any previous aircraft. A large aircraft (span was 51 ft 2¾ in [15.61 m]) of conventional de Havilland design and structure, the DH18 had accommo-

European air services in 1923-4. British Marine Air Navigation Company (BMAN) linked Southampton with the Channel Isles and northern France. Besides British companies French, German, Dutch and Spanish airlines linked Europe as far as Casablanca

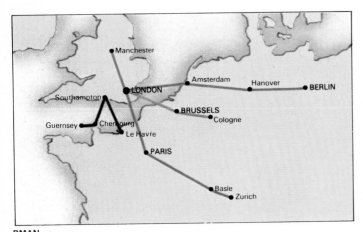

BMAN ━━━━━
DAIMLER ━━━━━
HANDLEY PAGE ━━━━━
INSTONE ━━━━━

dation for eight passengers in a cabin located immediately behind the engine in a fuselage that filled the gap between the upper and lower wings. Two passengers sat with their backs to the engine, another two at the rear of the cabin facing forward, and the other four in single seats on each side of the cabin, the port pair facing aft. The pilot occupied an open cockpit behind the upper wing. Power was provided by the 450-hp (336-kW) Napier Lion, which gave the DH18 a cruising speed of 100 mph (161 km/h) and a range of 400 miles (645 km). Without passengers, the DH18 was capable of carrying up to 2200 lb (998 kg) of freight, though performance was reduced from that attainable with passengers.

The other two main protagonists in the development of airliners in the UK in the aftermath of World War I were Handley Page and Vickers. Inevitably, both companies started with conversions of their military aircraft. The largest of the two aircraft produced by the two companies was the Handley Page V/1500 bomber, powered by a quartet of engines (375-hp/278-kW Rolls-Royce Eagle VIII, 400-hp/298-kW Liberty 12, 450-hp/336-kW Napier Lion, or 500-hp/373-kW Galloway Atlantic) and capable of carrying a military load of some 7500 lb (3400 kg). However, only three quasi-civil conversions of the V/1500 were made, and none of these entered service as airliners. Handley Page pinned greater faith in the twin-engined type, the classic type for conversion being the O/400 bomber, which had served with distinction during the war. At the end of the war, Handley Page was able to buy from the government 16 O/400s still in his factory, four of them finished and the other 12 still under construction. With commercial flying impossible as the Defence of the Realm Act reserved all flying to the military, Handley Page realized that he had a little time in which to produce adequate conversions for service after the Air Navigation Bill became law, in the event on 27 February, 1919, though the necessary Air Navigation Regulations could not be promulgated until later, delaying the start of internal British services until 1 May, 1919, and international operations until 25 August of the same year, when both

Aircraft Travel and Transport Company and Handley Page Transport Ltd started their services to Paris.

Handley Page at first envisaged an O/400 conversion with up to 16 passengers, but in the event the three conversion types carried fewer people. First came the O/7 (originally O/700), with fuselage fuel tanks replaced by tankage in extended engine nacelles, and accommodation for ten passengers in the main cabin in two facing rows each of five wicker seats, plus another two passengers in a nose cockpit fitted with windscreens and a raised coaming. It was this type which inaugurated Handley Page Transport's Paris service, though the flight had to leave from Hounslow rather than the Handley Page field at Cricklewood as customs facilities were only available at Hounslow. The O/7 aircraft were followed by the O/11, intended mainly for mail and cargo carrying, but with accommodation for three passengers at the rear of the cargo bay and two more passengers in the nose cockpit. With an increase in passenger demand, some of the O/11s were converted to O/7 standard as O/10s, with seating inside for ten, and windows along the full length of the passenger cabin. Powered by 360-hp (269-kW) Rolls-Royce Eagle VIII engines, the three types of the O series spanned 100 ft (30.5 m), had a speed of 97 mph (156 km/h) and possessed an endurance of 7h 30 min. A crew of two was carried. At the same time, several O/400 bombers were converted for civil use, being distinguishable from their custom-built civil counterparts by their convex roofs over the passenger accommodation, made necessary by the downward slope of the upper longerons on the rear fuselage of the military O/400.

Like de Havilland, Handley Page had realized from the earliest stages of postwar civil aviation that conversions of wartime aircraft could serve a useful purpose in the short term, but that once the demand for passenger flying had been stimulated and started on the path to growth, purpose-built commercial aircraft would be essential. For although large military aircraft were good load-carriers, their operating costs were generally high compared with the requirements of the civil market. Further stimulus in this direction was provided by the announcement of the First International Air Transport Exhibition, to be held at Amsterdam in August 1919.

The result of Handley Page's deliberations was an aircraft designed specifically as an airliner, but embodying much of the design concept and features of the earlier O/400 and V/1500 bombers. The concept was proved in a prototype designated W/400, and the production series became the W8. But although the type received its certificate of airworthiness on 7 August, 1920, no commercial services could at first be undertaken as the only two Napier Lion engines available were on loan from the Air Ministry, which would not allow their use for profit. Moreover, the French airlines with which Handley Page would be competing were supported by government subsidies, which allowed them to charge only half the economic fare over the Paris to London route.

The combination of these factors compelled Handley Page to look again at the project, with a view to using more economical engines and boosting accommodation if possible. The result was the W8b, powered by a pair of Rolls-

Royce Eagle VIII engines, which could carry between 12 and 14 passengers at 104 mph (167 km/h) for 500 miles (805 km). When fitted with the more powerful Eagle IX engine, the type became the W8c, able to carry up to 16 passengers at the same speed and over the same range as the W8b. In these two models the smart round windows of the W8 were replaced by rectangular units stretching along the passenger cabin, which had two rows of comfortable wicker armchairs and overhead racks for hand luggage and coats. Total production of the W8 series amounted to 22 civil examples, 11 of these being built in Belgium in SABCA for the Belgian flag-carrier SABENA. In service the type proved successful, and the last was not retired from an Indian summer's career of joy-riding flights until at least 1932. It is interesting to note that the civil W8 also gave rise to the Hyderabad heavy bomber and transport for the RAF, and to the W8e and W8f Hamilton airliners, the W9a Hampstead airliner, and the W10 airliner. The W8e and W8f were trimotor conversions of the basic W8 type, the two Siddeley Puma inlines in the wing nacelles being supplemented by a Rolls-Royce Eagle IX in the nose, to carry 12 passengers at 103 mph (166 km/h) over 500 miles (805 km); the W9a was powered by three radial engines, either Armstrong Siddeley Jaguar IVs or Bristol Jupiter VIs, and could carry 14 passengers at 114 mph (183 km/h) over a range of 400 miles (645 km); and the W10 was powered by two Napier Lion IIB inlines, giving the aircraft a speed of 100 mph (161 km/h) with 16 passengers over a range of 500 miles (805 km). Production of the W8e totalled 11 (ten of them built by SABCA), and all were used by SABENA; W8f production was three aircraft, one for Imperial Airways and two for SABENA, the latter again being built by SABCA. (These production figures are included in the total W8 production figures above.) Only one W9a was built for Imperial Airways, and four W10s were also built for the same airline, which was formed in 1924 as the British national flag-carrier by the merger of Handley Page Transport, British Marine Air Navigation, Daimler Hire and Instone Air Line, the four largest British airlines after the demise of Aircraft Transport and Travel in 1920.

The third company involved in airline production immediately after World War I was Vickers, with the Vimy Commercial derivative of the Vimy bomber just too late to see service in the war. Unlike de Havilland and Handley Page, the Vickers designers did not merely modify the standard bomber by the elimination of internal cross bracing to provide a passenger cabin, but instead produced a new fuselage design intended to supply generous seating room for the passengers. The new fuselage was of oval section, and well streamlined with a covering of sewn plywood to provide a semimonocoque structure. The new section ended just aft of the wings, where the original Vimy fuselage was bolted to the new section, the rear fuselage being faired out into the revised section with plywood formers and stringers, covered in fabric. The flying surfaces were the same as those of the bomber, and the long skid under the nose of the military variant was replaced by a single wheel to prevent the aircraft nosing over on landing. A crew of two was carried, and passenger seating for ten was standard, each seat having its own window. With the seats removed, the Vimy Commercial could carry 2500 lb (1135 kg) of freight. A notably advanced feature was the inbuilt airstep door, towards the back of the passenger saloon on the port side. Powered by a pair of 360-hp (269-kW) Rolls-Royce Eagle VIII inline engines, the Vimy Commercial had a top speed of 103 mph (165 km/h) and a range of 450 miles (724 km). Despite these advantages, the Vimy Commercial did not enjoy any great popularity as a Western airliner, largely because its bluff lines led to a rapid reduction in range when flying into a headwind, which meant that refuelling stops had to be made even on flights from London to Paris; the success of the type was assured, however, when the Chinese government ordered 40 Vimy Commercials, which were built between April 1920 and February 1921. Apart from the prototype, only three other Vimy Commercials were built: one for Instone Air Line, one for Grands Express Aériens, and one (a hybrid with Vickers Vernon features and Napier Lion engines) for the USSR, where it was used by the Red Air Fleet and then by the Soviet state airline Dobrolet from 1924. The importance of the Vimy Commercial lies in the fact that it established the design precedent of a high-capacity oval-section fuselage used in a number of Vickers transports in the 1920s and early 1930s. The first of these was the Vernon, followed by the Vulcan, Victoria Valentia and Vanguard.

Between the end of World War I and the signing of the Treaty of Versailles, the Germans also tried to develop ex-military types as commercial passenger carriers, but only with very limited success. Several companies which had been involved in the wartime *Riesenflugzeug* (giant aircraft) programme tried to attract interest in civil versions of their bombers, the most active concerns being Aviatik, DFW and Linke-Hoffman, but no orders were forthcoming. However, a few survivors from the war were used for commercial purposes, the most notable being the Zeppelin Staaken R.VI used for joy-rides over Berlin, the Zeppelin Staaken 8301 and 8303 seaplanes used for the carriage of up to 24 passengers each on week-end flights between the Havel lakes outside Berlin and Swinemünde on the Baltic coast, and the Zeppelin Staaken R.XIVa used for a few commercial passenger flights.

It was in Europe, though, that commercial aviation gathered the most immediate momentum, two manufacturers swiftly gaining positions of great dominance. These were the German firm Junkers and the Dutch firm Fokker. Both firms decided to capitalize on their wartime experience with aircraft design and manufacture, but without any suitable types for conversion into civilian transports, Junkers and Fokker opted to concentrate on the development of small single-engined aircraft with a limited passenger capacity.

The origins of the Junkers F 13 (originally J.13), which is now recognized as the world's first true airliner in the modern concept of the word, go back to February 1910, when Junkers patented his concept of 'an aircraft consisting of one wing, accommodating all components, engines, crew, passengers, fuel and structure' – in short a passenger-carrying flying-wing of cantilever construction. An aircraft conforming to the patent never emerged from the Junkers factories, but the patent marks the formal begin-

JUNKERS F 13a

Type: single-engined short-range transport
Powerplant: one 185-hp BMW IIIa
Accommodation: two crew and four passengers

Dimensions: length 31 ft 6 in (9.6 m); span 58 ft 2¾ in (17 m)
Weights: empty 2535 lb (1149.8 kg); loaded 3814 lb (1729 kg)

Performance: maximum speed 110 mph (177 km/h); cruising speed 87 mph (140 km/h); range 435 miles (700 km)

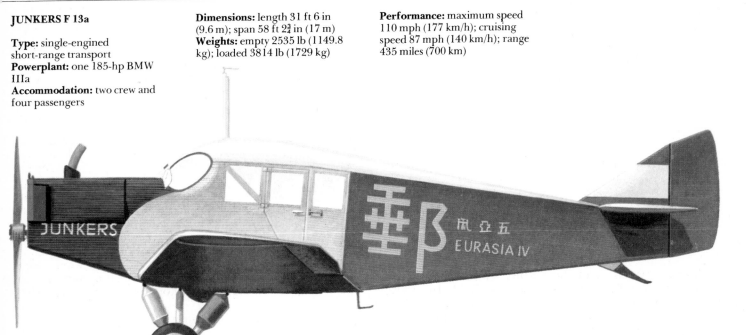

ning of the thick-section cantilever wing that marked all Junkers aircraft up to the middle of the 1930s. Junkers was equally convinced of the merits of metal as the primary structural material for aircraft, and in 1915 there appeared the J.1, a low-wing monoplane of cantilever construction, with iron and steel as the main structural materials. Despite successful flight trials, the J.1 was felt to be too heavy: Junkers agreed to a certain extent, but it was 1917 before the J.4 appeared. This was a sesquiplane ground-attack aircraft with cantilever wings and the light alloy duralumin as the main structural material. Corrugated duralumin skinning was also employed for the first time, and this too was to become a feature of Junkers aircraft until the middle of the 1930s. The J.4 entered service as the J I during the summer of 1917 and soon proved itself a useful and extremely strong aircraft. During 1917, though, there appeared more prophetic aircraft, the J.7 and J.9 prototypes for the D I monoplane fighter. With conventional Junkers construction of duralumin, corrugated skinning and a wing structure built up of a multitude of spars, these two aircraft reverted to the configuration of the earlier J.1 and J.2, setting the precedent followed by the two-seat J.10 (service designation CL I) and J.11 (service designation CLS I) of World War I and the J.13 (F 13) which first flew on 25 June 1919.

The J.13 was basically a scaled-up J.10, with a wing built up on the basis of nine dural spars braced by welded dural tubes. The aircraft had a distinctly advanced look to it, with the pilots' cockpit faired into the front of the passenger accommodation section, capable of taking four people in some comfort. The first example was powered by the 160-hp (119-kW) Mercedes D.IIIa inline engine, but production aircraft switched to the 185-hp (138-kW) BMW IIIa. Despite the fact that this engine gave only 25 hp (18.7 kW) more than the Mercedes engine, performance was improved markedly thanks to the BMW's far superior performance at altitude. The F 13 spanned 58 ft 2¾ in (17.75 m), and weighed 3814 lb (1730 kg) at take-off; performance was not in any way superior to that of contemporary British airliners (cruising speed 87 mph [140 km/h] and range about 435 miles [700 km]) but where

the F 13 really scored was in its modern appearance, great reliability, and evident structural strength. At the time the problem of fatigue was little understood, but the multiple redundancy of the F 13's structure meant that it remained in service far longer than all its later contemporaries, which had wing structures based on the use of only a few spars.

The success of the F 13 may be gauged quite simply by comparing the numbers built with the production records of its competitors. The exact figure is not known, but recent research in the archives of Messerschmitt-Bölkow-Blohm, which incorporates the old Junkers concern, indicates that about 450 were built. For the time this was a prodigious number, indicating the extent to which European airlines were dependent on the type. The largest single user was Junkers Luftverkehr, which operated more than 60 of the type between 1921 and 1926, when the company was absorbed in the new German state flag-carrier Deutsche Luft Hansa (later Deutsche Lufthansa, and finally Lufthansa). The Junkers Luftverkehr F 13s transported just under 282 000 passengers in the course of flying some 9 320 000 miles (15 000 000 km). Five years after the absorption of Junkers Luftverkehr, Deutsche Luft Hansa was still operating 43 F 13s – and at the same time another seven European airlines were operating a further 43 F 13s. Such was the sturdiness and versatility of the design (60-70 variants were produced on wheel, ski and float undercarriages).

The Fokker equivalent to the F 13 was of typical Reinhold Platz design: the F II, designed at Schwerin in Germany before Fokker left the country for his native Netherlands, with a welded steel-tube fuselage and high-set, unbraced wooden cantilever monoplane wing of considerable thickness : chord ratio. The open cockpit, under the wing leading edge, seated the pilot and an engineer or passenger, while behind this there was an enclosed cabin for four passengers; the fuselage was deep, terminating at its aft end in a vertical knife edge to which was hinged the small balanced rudder; large, overhanging balanced ailerons were located at each wing tip; and the whole machine sat on a somewhat ungainly steel-tube undercarriage located directly under the wing. The F II first flew in

A Fokker F-VIIb in service with
KLM. Fokker tri-motors
pioneered air routes in Europe
and the American continents

October 1919, and was powered by the excellent 185-hp (138-kW) BMW IIIa. The F II's gross weight was slightly greater than that of the F 13, at 4178 lb (1895 kg), but was much slower than the Junkers machine, its cruising speed being 75 mph (120 km/h), some 22 mph (35 km/h) less than the cruising speed of the Junkers F 13. About 30 Fokkers F IIs were built at Schwerin and sold to a number of the many airlines which sprang up in Germany immediately after World War I, and the Dutch national airline, KLM, also bought two.

With the F II, Fokker was well launched on a successful career as a builder of commercial aircraft. In 1920, therefore, the firm followed up the popularity of the F II by introducing the slightly large F III, which featured a wider fuselage to carry five passengers in the cabin, and a span of 57 ft 9 in (17.6 m) compared with the F II's 56 ft 7 in (17.25 m). An oddity of the design was that the pilot sat to the right of the 230-hp (172-kW) Siddeley Puma engine; but when the 360-hp (269-kW) Rolls-Royce Eagle was adopted in 1922 for late production models, the pilot's position was changed to the left. Some 40 F IIIs were built by Fokker, most with Siddeley and Rolls-Royce engines, but some with 350-hp (261-kW) BMW units. An unknown number of F IIIs with 185-hp (138-kW) BMW engines was also built under licence in Germany by Grulich.

Fokker then overestimated the European market for larger passenger aircraft, and produced the F IV, capable of accommodating ten passengers. Appearing in 1921, the F IV found no civil buyers, the only two sales being made to the US Army Air Service, which designated their 420-hp (313-kW) Liberty-powered aircraft T-2s. Fokker enjoyed even less success with the single F V of 1922: this was designed to fill the gap between the five-seat F III and the ten-seat F IV, and housed eight passengers in the fuselage, which was covered with plywood instead of the fabric of earlier types. Power was provided by a neatly cowled 360-hp (269-kW) Rolls-Royce Eagle, but performance was no better than that of older Fokker airliners. The oddest feature of the type was the fact that it was easily convertible from monoplane to biplane configuration and vice versa: for a full load the simply-detached cantilever lower wing was used, while for better performance at reduced weights this was detached to allow the type to operate as a monoplane, with a top speed of 109 mph (175 km/h) compared with the biplane's 93 mph (150 km/h). The F V is notable in the development of Fokker airliners, however, for the introduction of plywood covering for the fuselage, and a far higher standard of passenger comfort and luggage stowage than in earlier models.

The next Fokker airliner was the classic F VII, one of the truly great aircraft of all time. (The F VI was a fighter, given the prefix letter F at the express request of the US Army Air Service to mark it as a fighter.) The F VII eventually ran to a series of eight sub-types, with widely differing powerplants and capabilities, and the original F VII appeared in 1924. After the failure of the F V, the F VII reverted to the earlier Fokker practice of a fabric-covered fuselage, and though the influence of Platz could still be strongly seen, the F VII was in fact designed by H Rethel, latterly chief designer of the German firm Kondor. The one notable departure from earlier Fokker aircraft was the excellent wide-span undercarriage: previous Fokker aircraft had used the 'conventional' type with the open ends of the Vs attached to the lower longerons, and the apices braced apart by the continuous axle mounting the twin wheels. This was adequate in small aircraft, but provided too narrow a track for larger aircraft. Rethel's concept therefore provided for a split-axle undercarriage type made up of numerous steel tubes.

Only eight of the original F VII type were built, all for

KLM, with power provided by a single 360-hp (269-kW) Rolls-Royce Eagle or 450-hp (336-kW) Napier Lion inline.

In service the F VII soon proved its worth, but the type was slightly underpowered, and it was clear that the undercarriage produced considerable drag, keeping maximum speed down to 96 mph (155 km/h). A company pilot, Hubertus Grasé, suggested considerable improvements to the undercarriage, and these were soon implemented on the F VIIA: twin steel-tube Vs were hinged at their open ends to the lower longerons, while the outboard apices held the wheels. Springing was provided within the oleo part of the main support member running vertically upwards to the wing main spar. The fuselage was also cleaned up aerodynamically, and the balanced ailerons were replaced by plain units giving the wing tips a rounded contour. Just as importantly, provision was made in the design of the fuselage nose for the mounting of any one of the growing number of radial engines coming onto the market: these air-cooled units had proved themselves admirable engines, with great reliability, good fuel consumption, ease of mounting, high power and low weight as they did not need the radiator, water and associated 'plumbing' of inline engines. The one real disadvantage of the radial, compared with the inline, was considerably higher drag, though this was to be improved with the later introduction of close cowlings of the Townend ring and NACA types. The F VIIA could also accommodate inline engines, and the nose structure was stressed to accept engines of between 350 hp (261 kW) and 525 hp (392 kW). Introduced in 1925, the F VIIA soon proved itself a first-class machine: maximum speed with the 480-hp (358-kW) Bristol Jupiter radial was 118 mph (190 km/h), while operating costs were low thanks to the sturdiness of the design and user airlines' ability to fit the engine of their choice. Fokker built 42 F VIIAs, and the type was also widely built under licence in other countries.

Further success was yet to come to the F VII, however, with the introduction of the F VIIA-3m tri-motor variant. Appearing in 1925 as a single conversion of an otherwise standard F VIIA, the first F VII-3m was converted in the space of two months by Reinhold Platz to accommodate two additional engines mounted on the main undercarriage legs under the wings. The object was to ensure success in the Ford Reliability Tour, a 1900-mile (3060-km) competition being organized by the car magnate Henry Ford to stimulate the growth of civil aviation in the USA in 1925. Powered by three 240-hp (179-kW) Wright Whirlwind radials, the F VII-3m proved to have a top speed of 118 mph (190 km/h), the same as that of the F VIIA with only two-thirds of the power, but the company's belief in the reliability of the tri-motor layout was soon vindicated, the Fokker aircraft excelling in the competition by virtue of its speed, economy, versatility and ability at times to fly on a single engine. From this time on, therefore, Fokker built all F VIIAs with provision for the mounting of an additional two engines should the operator so require. This made the basic F VIIA extremely popular. Most operators used their aircraft in tri-motor configuration with Wright Whirlwinds or 220-hp (164-kW) Armstrong Siddeley Lynx radials, and the type was also in great demand for long-range flights of the route-proving and record-breaking variety. The single F VIIA-3m/M was an experimental bomber version with external bomb racks under the fuselage and other military fittings. Including the later Fokker F VIIB-3m, some 116 tri-motor F VIIs were built by Fokker.

Although heavy commercial load-carriers of some importance were being planned in the UK during the mid-1920s, the only other major type to enter service during the early part of the decade was the de Havilland DH34, the direct result of early operations with converted military aircraft: the lesson learned by the now defunct Aircraft Transport and Travel firm was that the only way to operate economically was to carry more passengers at higher speeds at a lower specific fuel consumption than was possible with conversions. In short, the lesson was the need to carry more payload per unit of power. De Havilland had already started moving in this direction with the unsuccessful ten-seat DH29, but now started work on a new design after consultation with various possible user airlines.

The result was the DH34, which incorporated many of the better features of the DH29, but used a biplane configuration in place of the earlier machine's monoplane layout. Another notable feature was the use of hinged access panels for the 450-hp (336-kW) Napier Lion engine: these swung down to the horizontal position when opened, providing the ground crew with ideally placed working platforms for maintenance, doing away with the need for ladders, platforms and the like at airports. An inertia starter was also provided for the engine, doing away with the need for swinging the propeller to start the engine. This feature was thus used for the first time on a civil aircraft, and soon became standard on all commercial aircraft. The Lion engine was installed in a detachable unit, complete with its cooling system, allowing the whole powerplant to be changed with great ease. The DH34 carried ten passengers, and at a cruising speed of 105 mph (169 km/h) had a range of 365 miles (587 km). Though a successful design by British standards, the state of British airliner design is reflected in the fact that only 11 DH34s were built, six going to Daimler Hire, four to Instone Air Line and one to the Soviet state airline Dobrolet.

In Italy, postwar transformations had been made of fairly large numbers of the multi-engined Caproni bombers produced in that country for service with the Italian, French and US air services. Some Ca 1 and Ca 3 aircraft were thus modified, with passenger accommodation for six: typical was the Ca 56a of 1919, modified from a number of Ca 3 variants, with three 150-hp (112-kW) Isotta-Fraschini V.4B inline engines. With a span of 74 ft 7¼ in (22.74 m), the Ca 56a had a speed of only 81 mph (130 km/h). Another conversion was the Ca 57 of 1919, derived from airframes of the Ca 5 basic type, able to carry eight passengers at between 81 and 93 mph (130 and 150 km/h) depending on the engines fitted: three 200-hp (149-kW) Fiat A.12, 250-hp (187-kW) Isotta-Fraschini V.6 or 300-hp (224-kW) Fiat A.12bis inline engines. Other notable Caproni airliners were the Ca 48, also of 1919, able to carry up to 23 passengers in a large cabin filling the space between the middle and lower wings of this large triplane powered by three 360-hp (269-kW) Liberty engines and capable of speeds of up to 87 mph (140 km/h); and the Ca 59 of 1920.

Adolescent airliners

By the middle of the 1920s, airline development had crystallized the need for two types of airliner: single-engined aircraft with seating for up to about eight passengers, and multi-engined aircraft able to accommodate up to about 15 passengers. In both cases ranges rarely exceeded 500 miles (805 km), and a cruising speed of about 100 mph (161 km/h) was adjudged adequate. The single-engined market was well catered for by the Junkers F 13 and several of the earlier Fokker types, and the best early expression of the multi-engined concept is to be found in the definitive Fokker F VIIB-3m of 1928. This was basically an updated F VIIA-3m, modified at the request of the polar explorer Sir Hubert Wilkins to incorporate longer-span wings for extra range. The US Army also ordered the new type with further improvements, and so was born the classic F VIIB-3m. Power was generally provided by three 300-hp (224-kW) Wright Whirlwind radials, although other favoured engines were the Armstrong Siddeley Lynx, Gnome-Rhône Titan and the Walter Castor. With the Whirlwind engines, the F VIIB-3m had a maximum speed of 130 mph (210 km/h) compared with the F VIIA-3m's 118 mph (190 km/h), despite the fact that the wing span had been increased from 63 ft 4 in (19.3 m) to 71 ft 2 in (21.7 m), and gross weight from 8818 lb (4000 kg) to 11 464 lb (5200 kg). The F VIIB-3m proved the most popular of all the Fokker airliners, and was used extensively as an executive aircraft and also as a record-breaking machine in the hands of men such as Sir Charles Kingsford-Smith. The Fokker F VIIB-3m also has the distinction of having made the first regular commercial flights by a US airline to a foreign destination, when the fledgling Pan American company started flights between Key West in Florida and Havana in Cuba in October 1927, shortly after commercial airline operations became permitted under US law. It is impossible to differentiate in production records between the F VIIA-3m and the F VIIB-3m, total production of the two types running to 116 Dutch-built examples.

By the mid-1920s the tri-motor layout had established itself as standard for multi-engined airliners, offering the

A Ford Tri-motor, the reliable and popular transport of the 20s and 30s

FORD 4-AT-E

Type: three-engined medium-range transport
Powerplant: three 300-hp Wright Whirlwind J-6-9 radials
Accommodation: two crew and 11 passengers

Dimensions: span 74 ft (22.5 m); length 49 ft 10 in (15.16 m)
Weights: empty 6500 lb (2948.3 kg); loaded 10 130 lb (4594.8 kg)
Performance: cruising speed 107 mph (172 km/h); range 570 miles (917 km)

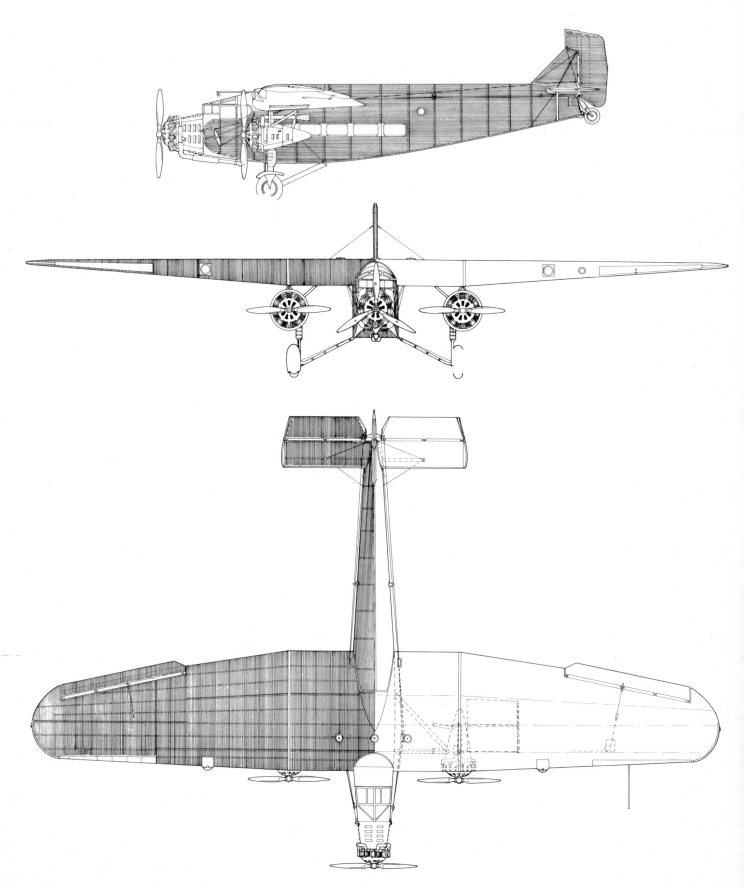

Mechanics at work in the USA;
they are servicing Ford and
Fokker short-range airliners.
Fokker aircraft were built under
licence in the United States

safety of a multi-engined powerplant disposition without the structural and allied problems bedevilling the design of four-engined tractor aircraft. Notable amongst these tri-motors were two other monoplanes (the Ford 4-AT and the Junkers G 31) and two biplanes (the Armstrong Whitworth Argosy and the de Havilland DH66 Hercules). Appearing in 1926, a year after the Fokker F VIIA-3m, the Junkers G 31 was powered by three 450-hp (336-kW) radial engines, and could carry 16 passengers at a cruising speed of 90 mph (145 km/h). The G 31 was largely derived from the successful G 23 and G 24, of which some 70 had been built. And just as the G 31 was an enlarged version of the G 24, intended to supplement and then replace the earlier machine, the W 33 was intended as a replacement for the F 13. Appearing in 1926, the W 33 followed the traditional Junkers design philosophy of metal structure, corrugated skinning, and low-wing monoplane configuration, and was powered by a single 310-hp (231-kW) Junkers L 5 inline engine in its primary role of light freighting. The W 34, which also appeared in 1926, was in essence a slightly scaled-up W 33, and intended for passenger operations: span was increased by $28\frac{1}{3}$ in (72 cm) to 60 ft $7\frac{1}{2}$ in (18.48 m), but power was more than doubled by the fitting of a 660-hp (492-kW) BMW 132A radial or other radial of similar power. With a crew of two and six passengers, the W 34 proved an ideal supplement to the F 13, maximum speed being a very respectable 165 mph (265 km/h) and range the fairly standard 559 miles (900 km). Production of the W 33 totalled 199, while that of the W 34 reached 1791 examples (including the K 43 light bomber derivative).

Generally referred to only as the Ford Tri-motor, this important aircraft was in fact the Ford Model 4-AT in its most successful form. The origins of the design lay in the 2-AT mailplane of 1925, designed by William B Stout of the Stout Metal Airplane Company. Powered by a single Liberty inline engine, the 2-AT caught the attention of Henry Ford, who was seeking to diversify his interests from the automobile industry. Ford bought the Stout company, but after the failure of the 3-AT sacked Stout and brought in his own chief engineer in the form of Howard Hicks. The 3-AT was essentially the 2-AT with a larger wing and the single Liberty inline replaced by a trio of 200-hp (149-kW) Wright J-4 radials, and was surely one of the most ungainly aircraft every produced. The fuselage had a nose of considerable height, with the pilot perched in an open cockpit on the top, the front windows of the passenger compartment running right round the centre of the front, and one of the engines mounted in the chin position. The other two engines were located in front of the wing leading edge.

Hicks immediately began work on a new design, which appeared in 1926 as the 4-AT. This combined the basic configuration of the Fokker tri-motors, the structure of the Junkers airliners, and the mass production building techniques of the US car industry: the result was one of the world's most successful aircraft, flown by more than 100 airlines, and still in fairly widespread service in the late 1970s as a freighter in several Central and South American countries. Extraordinarily for an aircraft of its size and weight, the 4-AT is highly manoeuvrable and has been

snap-rolled and looped. The versatility of the type was also enhanced by the fact that wheel, ski and float undercarriages could be fitted, as with many other airliners of the period.

The first few 4-ATs had an open cockpit, somewhat ungainly undercarriages and the exhaust gases collected from each underwing engine in a collector ring before being piped through the wing to exhaust on the upper surface. But the definitive model of the 4-AT family was the 4-AT-B, and larger and more substantial aircraft than the basic 4-AT. Powered by three 220-hp (164-kW) Wright Whirlwind radials, the 4-AT-B carried up to 14 passengers at a cruising speed of 100 mph (161 km/h) over a range of 570 miles (917 km). The first operator of the type was the Ford Motor Company, on 2 August, 1926, but soon the type was in ever widening service, largely with Stout Air Services and Maddux Air Lines. (In November 1929 Maddux merged with Transcontinental Air Transport to form Transcontinental and Western Air, the precursor of today's TWA when TAT merged with Western Air Express in July 1930.) At the time of Maddux's takeover, the airline was operating eight 4-ATs and seven 5-ATs, this making it the largest single operator of the Ford tri-motors at the time. Some 78 Ford 4-ATs were built, though production of the basic type continued with the 5-AT.

The Ford 5-AT appeared in the summer of 1928 as a result of the appearance of the excellent Pratt & Whitney Wasp radial of 420 hp (313 kW). This was basically the 4-AT with a larger wing (span was 77 ft 10 in [23.72 m] compared with 74 ft [22.56 m]), greater fuel capacity and accommodation for up to 16 passengers. The importance of the Wasp engine is apparent by a simple comparison between the performance of the 4-AT-E (300-hp [224-kW] Wright J-6) and of the 5-AT-C (420-hp [313-kW] Pratt & Whitney Wasp): maximum speed of the two types was 130 mph (209 km/h) and 135 mph (217 km/h), cruising speed 107 mph (172 km/h) and 112 mph (180 km/h), and range 570 miles (917 km) compared with 510 miles (821 km); but

Below: A US-built Fokker F-10A. The first US operator was Western Air Express who brought them into service in November 1928. The F-10A could carry 14 passengers up to 800 miles (1287 km)

Right: A Bellanca CH-300 Pacemaker winched up a slipway in a coastal town in Alaska. Many prewar aircraft are still in use as private owner or passenger-carrying aircraft

while performances remained relatively comparable, the 5-AT-C carried a payload of 3743 lb (1698 kg) compared with the earlier type's 1275 lb (782 kg), and handling was made safer by the slight improvement in power loading. Total production of the 5-AT series reached 116 aircraft, the last model being the 5-AT-D of 1931, with increased head-room in the passenger cabin. As important as the performance and payload of the 4-AT and 5-AT was the longevity and general safety of the Ford airliner. Although problems were encountered if one of the wing engines failed, the Ford tri-motors acquired an excellent record for safety in all conditions, and the use of Alclad for the skinning has led to the type outlasting its anticipated 2500 hr flying life by very considerable margins, thanks to the strength and corrosion-resistance of the Alclad.

The appearance of the Pratt & Whitney Wasp radial is also of singular importance: hitherto Wright had dominated the market for radial engines, but the Wasp and later Pratt & Whitney designs produced an extremely healthy competition in the US radial engine market. This led to the swift development of these types in power, reliability and fuel consumption, to the extent that they came virtually to drive inline engines off the US market. It is interesting to note that the driving force of Pratt & Whitney were two ex-employees of the Wright company, Frederick Rentschler and George Mead, who had broken away to form their own firm in 1925.

The first US civil user of the now legendary Wasp was the Boeing 40, which first entered service in July 1927 with Boeing Air Transport. Designed principally as a mail carrier, but with spartan accommodation for two passengers, the biplane Boeing 40 set new standards in economy and performance, largely as a result of careful design and the use of the Wasp engine. Cruising speed was 110 mph (177 km/h) and range 300 miles (483 km), which was improved upon by the introduction of the Boeing 40B in September 1929. Powered by the 525-hp (392-kW) Pratt & Whitney Hornet radial, the Boeing 40B could carry up to three passengers at a cruising speed of 125 mph (201 km/h) over a range of 535 miles (861 km). Total production of the two types was 82 aircraft. The only other US airliners of the period to enter widespread production were the Bellanca Pacemaker CH-300, which could carry

six passengers at a cruising speed of 122 mph (196 km/h) over a range of 675 miles (1086 km) on the 220 hp (164 kW) of its Wright Whirlwind radial (an oddity of this and other Bellanca types was the use of large struts bracing the high monoplane wing, adding to the total lift by being faired to an aerofoil shape); the Buhl CA-3 Air Sedan, capable of carrying four passengers at a cruising speed of 110 mph (177 km/h) over a range of 800 miles (1287 km) on the 220 hp (164 kW) of its Wright Whirlwind, the aircraft having the low-drag and high-lift qualities inherent in its sesquiplane configuration; the Fairchild FC-2 and FC-2W with accommodation for four and six passengers respectively, carried over a range of 150 miles (241 km) at a cruising speed of 115 mph (185 km/h) on the power of a 220-hp (164-kW) Wright Whirlwind or 450-hp (336-kW) Pratt & Whitney Wasp; the magnificent Lockheed Vega monoplane, with seating for six passengers, a cruising speed of 135 mph (217 km/h), range of 600 miles (966 km) and power provided by a 420-hp (313-kW) Pratt & Whitney Wasp; the Stinson SM-1 Detroiter, with a 200-hp (149-kW) Wright Whirlwind carrying four passengers at a cruising speed of 105 mph (169 km/h) over a range of 550 miles (885 km); the Travel Air 6000, whose 220-hp (164-kW) Wright Whirlwind provided the motive power to move six passengers at a cruising speed of 100 mph (161 km/h) for 600 miles (966 km); and a number of Fokker aircraft.

Although Fokker had exported aircraft to the USA soon after the end of World War I, for a variety of reasons it became imperative to establish local design and manufacturing facilities in the USA, and between 1924 and 1932 Fokker subsidiaries in the USA included the Atlantic Aircraft Manufacturing Company, Fokker Aircraft Corporation and General Aviation Corporation. Under these guises the Fokker company produced a number of important civil aircraft. Numerically the most significant of these American Fokker airliners were the F 10 and 10A (65 and 59 built), the F 14 and 14A (35 built), the F 32 (10 built), the Universal or Model 4 (44 built), and the Super Universal or Model 8 (123 built). The earliest of these was the Universal, an airliner with seating for four passengers. Powered by a 220-hp (164-kW) Wright Whirlwind (later models having the uprated 300-hp [224-kW] version), the

FOKKER F 32

Type: four-engined medium-range transport
Powerplant: four 575-hp Pratt & Whitney Hornet
Accommodation: two crew and 32 passengers by day, with 16 in sleeper berths by night

Dimensions: span 99 ft (30 m); length 96.10 ft (29.5 m)
Weights: loaded 22 500 lb (10 205 kg); empty 14 200 lb (6440.9 kg)
Performance: max speed 140 mph (225.3 km/h)

Right: An early Fokker F 32

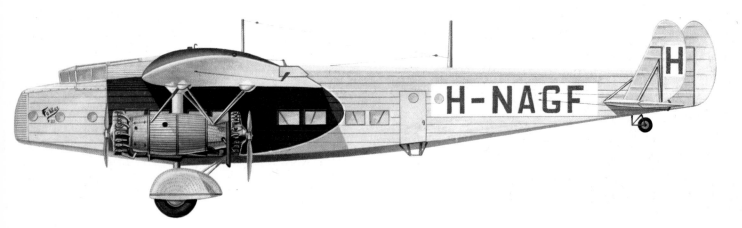

Universal entered service with Colonial Air Transport in 1926. Maximum speed was 130 mph (209 km/h), cruising speed 100 mph (161 km/h), and range 535 miles (861 km). Designed by R B C Noorduyn, the single-engined Universal proved particularly popular in remote areas. The design was improved in 1927 into the Super Universal, which was pioneered in service by Western Air Transport in August 1929. Early Universals had featured an open cockpit, but on the Super Universal this was fully enclosed, and power was provided by the 420-hp (313-kW) Pratt & Whitney Wasp. Span was increased by 35 in (88.9 cm) to 50 ft 8 in (15.44 m), and with a maximum of six passengers the Super Universal had a top speed of 138 mph (222 km/h), a cruising speed of 118 mph (190 km/h) and a range of 740 miles (1191 km). As with the Universal, the Super Universal could also be operated from floats, and was popular for operations of the 'bush' type. Of the 123 built, 29 were built in Japan by Nakajima, and 14 in Canada.

The F 10 and 10A appeared in 1927, being brought into service in May and November 1928 respectively by Western Air Express. The two aircraft were closely modelled on the Dutch F VII tri-motor series. The F 10, powered by three 425-hp (317-kW) Pratt & Whitney Wasps, had a span of 71 ft (21.64 m), and could carry 12 passengers at a cruising speed of 120 mph (193 km/h) over a range of 900 miles (1448 km); the F 10A was powered by the same type of engines, but had wings spanning 79 ft 2 in (24.13 m), and could carry 14 passengers at a cruising speed also of 120 mph (193 km/h) but over the reduced range of 800 miles (1287 km).

The F 14 and 14A appeared in 1929, with power provided by one 525-hp (392-kW) Pratt & Whitney Hornet (F 14) or 575-hp (429-kW) Pratt & Whitney Hornet radial. Western Air Express again pioneered the type in airline service, the first F 14 starting operations in December 1929, the F 14A early in 1930. Passenger accommodation in both models was eight, but with the more powerful engine the maximum speed was increased by 8 mph (187 km/h), and range was 730 miles (1175 km). Although the two models bore a marked resemblance to other Fokker airliners, they were notable for the fact that the monoplane wing was mounted above the fuselage on four short struts,

and the fact that the pilot's cockpit was positioned to the rear of the passenger compartment.

The F 32, which entered service with Western Air Express in April 1930, had first flown in 1929, and should logically have been designated F 12. However, Western Air Express asked for the number 32 to be inserted in the designation to indicate the type's maximum seating capacity (reduced to 16 for night operations with sleeper berths). The mounting of the four 575-hp (429-kW) Pratt & Whitney Hornet radials in two pairs (one tractor and one pusher in each pair) was a logical extension of the undercarriage main-leg mounting of the tri-motor types, but engine cooling for the rear units proved an insurmountable problem, resulting in the building of only ten examples of the type. Interestingly, soundproofing was performed by the inclusion of balsa wood into the fuselage walls.

By the middle of the 1920s, the UK was already beginning to fall back in the performance aspects of airliner design. With the newly-formed Imperial Airways dominating the civil aircraft market, it was inevitable that manufacturers should concentrate their efforts on types to meet the airline's peculiar requirements: despite the fact that the various companies that had been amalgamated to form Imperial Airways had enjoyed singular success on European routes, the new British flag-carrier immediately saw its role as a means of political and economic communication with the far-flung portions of the British empire, notably the dominions. With no opposition, therefore, the company chose to operate very comfortable, but also very slow, services to all parts of the empire: aircraft rarely flew stages of more than 375 miles (603 km), and passengers often had to travel by train or boat to the next stage of their journey. The two classic airliners to emerge from this period, however, were the Armstrong Whitworth Argosy and de Havilland DH66 Hercules.

The origins of the Argosy lay in a 1922 specification for a transport to operate on Middle Eastern routes, with three reliable radial engines and the ability to operate on 500-mile (805-km) stages against a 30-mph (48-km) headwind. However, in 1925 Imperial Airways were looking for a machine to operate on its longer European routes, and thought the Armstrong Whitworth 1922 proposal a likely

The Short L17 'Scylla' which
entered service with Imperial
Airways on their European
routes. 'Scylla' was wrecked in a
storm at Drem in Scotland in the
winter of 1940

A de Havilland 66 Hercules. 11 aircraft were built, seven of which went to Imperial Airways and the rest to Australia

Bottom: Armstrong Whitworth Argosy 'City of Birmingham' of the Imperial Airways in flight in the early 1930s. It carried 20 passengers with the pilot and first officer in an open cockpit

Right: A Short Calcutta flying boat moored on the Thames by the Houses of Parliament. The visit, which lasted for three days, began on August 1, 1928 and allowed MPs to examine the aircraft in detail

candidate. The airline accordingly ordered two Argosys, and the Air Ministry a third. As it eventually appeared in March 1926, the Argosy was a singularly unaesthetic aircraft, with a slab-sided fuselage, triple vertical tail surfaces, biplane wings and horizontal tail surfaces, and a stalky undercarriage. In general conformity with established British practice, the fuel tanks were located well away from the fuselage, in this instance two tanks being located in the centre section of the upper wing. The most ungainly aspect of the Argosy was its engine installation, in particular that of the third 385-hp (287-kW) Armstrong Siddeley Jaguar radial perched in front of the fuselage nose. The fuselage was of steel-tube construction, while the wings and tail surfaces were built up of wood, the whole being covered in doped fabric.

The first Argosy entered airline service in July 1926, and despite the comparative indifference of the performance (cruising speed of 95 mph [153 km/h] and range of about 330 miles [531 km]), the Argosy proved highly successful and popular: successful because costs per ton-mile fell from the 21p of the DH34 and 14p of the Handley Page W10 to a mere 9p; and popular because the accommodation of the Argosy was large and well provided with windows. The third aircraft, ordered by the Air Ministry, was handed over to Imperial Airways in March 1927.

So good had the performance of the Argosy been that in 1928 Imperial Airways ordered four more aircraft, of an improved standard designated Argosy Mark II. These aircraft had increased fuel tankage, giving a range of some 525 miles (845 km), geared Jaguar IVA engines developed 410 hp (306 kW) each (the Argosy Mark I's engines were of the direct-drive type), payload improved from 4500 lb

(2041 kg) to 5000 lb (2268 kg), Townend rings on the engines (these were soon stripped off), and automatic wing-tip slots on the upper wing to improve low-speed handling and hence safety at take-off and landing. Heating for the cabin was also provided by means of heater muffs and exhaust extension pipes from the fuselage engine.

The seven Argosys gave excellent service, the only fatal accident occurring on 28 March, 1933, when all three crew and 12 passengers were killed in a crash in Belgium. By 1936 the only survivor, after the type was retired from airline service, was used for joy-rides over Blackpool.

The first air routes to the East 1929-39. The airliner not only allowed the colonial powers of France, Britain and Holland to reach their colonies and mandates in the Middle East and beyond, it also allowed mail to move far faster than any maritime service. The first services were not entirely reliable, however, and sometimes the would-be traveller had to change aircraft at several points and even go on ships or by road along the route

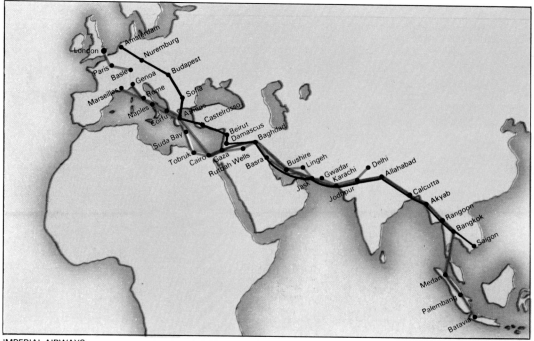

IMPERIAL AIRWAYS_____
KLM _____
AIR ORIENT _____

The DH66 Hercules was a contemporary and equivalent of the Argosy, but intended specifically for operations between Cairo and Karachi with mail, passengers and cargo. The route had originally been flown by DH10 Amiens bombers converted for the role by the RAF, but in 1925 it was decided that Imperial Airways would run the route with the aid of a substantial subsidy. A stringent requirement for the aircraft needed on the route was drawn up by Imperial Airways, its most important aspects being the need for multiple engines to minimize the chances of the aircraft being forced down by engine failure, and engines of considerable power for 'hot and high' conditions.

In concept the DH66 was quite similar to the Armstrong Whitworth Argosy, though of greater aesthetic appeal: the fuselage was of steel-tube construction, with wooden wings of biplane configuration, triple vertical tail surfaces, and biplane horizontal tail surfaces. The steel-tube fuselage had been chosen instead of the normal de Havilland structure of spruce structure with plywood covering because of the difficulties of obtaining spruce of the right lengths, and the suspect nature of plywood under hot operating conditions. The two pilots sat in an open cockpit on top of the forward fuselage, and the passenger and freight compartments were formed by two large plywood boxes mounted inside the steel-tube structure. As in other civil aircraft of British design, the fuel tanks were located in the centre section of the upper wing. Power was provided by three 420-hp (313-kW) Bristol Jupiter VI radials, one mounted in the fuselage nose and the other two in the lower wing leading edges under the first set of interplane struts. Passenger accommodation was restricted to seven seats by the large air mail compartment and the anticipated small demand for seats on the planned route.

The first example appeared in September 1926, and entered service in December 1926. The last of the five aircraft called for in Imperial Airways' order was delivered in March 1927, by which time the DH66 had already shown itself an excellent aircraft. Further production was assured in 1928 by an order for four examples by West Australian Airways, intended for service on the route

between Adelaide and Perth. These aircraft seated 14 passengers and less mail, and had an enclosed cockpit for the pilots. Such cockpit enclosures were subsequently retrofitted to Imperial Airways' first five DH66s, and became standard on the extra two aircraft later ordered by Imperial Airways as replacements for two crashed aircraft. The last two surviving machines were broken up in South Africa during 1943, after a successful and enterprising career, despite total production of only 11 aircraft of the type. The DH66 had a maximum speed of 128 mph (206 km/h) and a cruising speed of 110 mph (177 km/h).

The remarkable fact about the Armstrong Whitworth Argosy and DH66 Hercules is that they enjoyed careers as successful as they were. At a time when most other designers had opted for metal structures, or at least for plywood coverings, British designers were tied to the odd requirements of Imperial Airways, which stressed the importance of regularity of services rather than their speed. Typical of this approach is the service opened in 1929 between London and Karachi: the passenger first boarded an Argosy at Croydon (after a coach trip from London), and then flew to Paris and then on to Basle; here he boarded a train for Genoa, where he boarded a Short Calcutta flying boat for the trip across the Mediterranean to Alexandria; another change was then made, this time to a DH66 Hercules, which flew the passenger to Baghdad, down to the Persian Gulf, along the coast of Baluchistan and finally to Karachi after a trip of six days and a cost of £130 including meals and hotel accommodation. The same journey done by surface transportation took only two and half times longer.

With the advanced Fokker, Junkers, Ford and Lockheed aircraft now showing the way forward, it might have been expected that Imperial Airways would see the error of its ways, and appreciate that safety and regularity could be combined with speed. But this was not the case, as evidenced by the ordering in 1930 of one of the truly great biplane airliners, the Handley Page HP42 Hannibal and HP45 Heracles series.

The origins of the series lay in a 1928 Imperial Airways requirement for aircraft to replace the Armstrong Whit-

Left over from another era, a
Clipper of the Antilles Air Boat
service stands beached in the
early 1970s. Flying boats were the
pioneers of many of the
transatlantic and Pacific routes
now flown by jets

worth Argosy and DH66 Hercules. The airline issued its requirements to the whole British aircraft industry, asking for tenders to four different types: three-engined aircraft for service on European routes, and four-engined aircraft for service on routes to the Far East. Engines were preferably to be air-cooled radials, and would be supplied initially by British Airways, as would the lighting and radio equipment, and all types were to have low stalling speeds and standard ranges (300 miles [483 km] for European aircraft, and 500 miles [805 km] for Far Eastern aircraft). Handley Page tendered for all four types, and were extremely gratified to find that its tenders for the two four-engined types proved to be just what Imperial Airways wanted. The company received orders for four Eastern aircraft (company designation HP42) and four European aircraft (company designation HP45). For certification purposes the aircraft were treated as belonging to the same type, the HP42, with suffixes from -1 to -8. In charge of design was G R Volkert, and the aircraft he produced may be taken as the definitive expression of biplane airliner design: the fuselage consisted of a monocoque structure of mainly corrugated aluminium for its forward two-thirds, the tail being of welded steel tube with fabric covering; the sesquiplane wings were of standard metal construction with fabric covering, braced by Warren-girder struts to obviate the need for wires; the lower wing featured a pronounced anhedral on its panels inboard of the lower engine mountings to keep the undercarriage legs as short as possible, but yet permit the root fittings to be above the level of the cabin ceiling, so permitting an uninterrupted passenger accommodation space; and the four engines were arranged in as tight a cluster as possible with their blade tips only just clearing each other, two engines being located close to each other in the upper wing, and the other two engines below and outboard of these in the lower wing. To keep the passenger entrance as low as possible, the fuselage was sagged slightly, which led inevitably to the nickname 'The Flying Banana' being given to the type. Overall, the HP42/45 presented a decidedly obsolescent picture, but one nonetheless full of all the best features and dignity of the biplane configuration. Despite the fact that

the airline had called for two different ranges, a later amendment called for a uniform tankage of 500 Imp gal (2273 litres) in upper-wing tanks. Power was provided by the first-class Bristol Jupiter: the four European aircraft (designated HP42W by Imperial Airways and named Heracles, Horatius, Hengist and Helena) were powered by 555-hp (414-kW) Jupiter XFBMs; and the four Eastern aircraft (designated HP42E by Imperial Airways and named Hannibal, Hadrian, Hanno and Horsa) had the 555-hp (414-kW) Jupiter XI.

Under Volkert's supervision, most of the design work had been done by H D Boultbee, and both men were pleased by the general appearance and performance of the first example (G-AAGX Hannibal) when it made its maiden flight on 14 November, 1930. The type entered service with Imperial Airways in 1931. Each of the types carried a crew of four, with passenger accommodation for between 18 and 24 in the HP42, and for 38 in the HP45, the difference being accounted for by the increased mail-carrying provision of the HP42. In performance the two types were comparable on most counts: cruising speed was in the order of 90 mph (145 km/h), and range was about 500 miles (805 km). The one major performance difference was in top speed, which was 120 mph (193 km/h) in the HP42s and 127 mph (204 km/h) in the HP45s, despite the latter's greater all-up weight (29 500 lb [13 400 kg] as compared with 28 000 lb [12 700 kg]).

Even before its service entry the type was obsolescent compared with the latest German and Dutch monoplane airliners, but the eight aircraft soon acquired a well-deserved and enduring popularity with passengers and operators alike: the four-engined layout provided great reliability, the rugged construction allowed operations in remote areas without serious problems, and the cabin layout with good soundproofing and first-class catering facilities made journeys less tiresome than in more advanced aircraft. Seven of the eight were still operational at the beginning of World War II in September 1939, Hengist having been burned out in a hangar fire at Karachi in 1937 after alteration for Eastern use. The seven survivors were used as troop transports in World War II,

HANDLEY PAGE HP 45

Type: four-engined medium-range transport
Powerplant: (HP 42W) four 555-hp Bristol Jupiter XFBM radials
Accommodation: two crew and 38 passengers

Dimensions: span 130 ft (39.6 m); length 89 ft 9 in (27.2 m)
Weights: all up 29 500 lb (13 380 kg)
Performance: maximum speed 127 mph (204 km/h); cruising speed 100 mph (160 km/h)

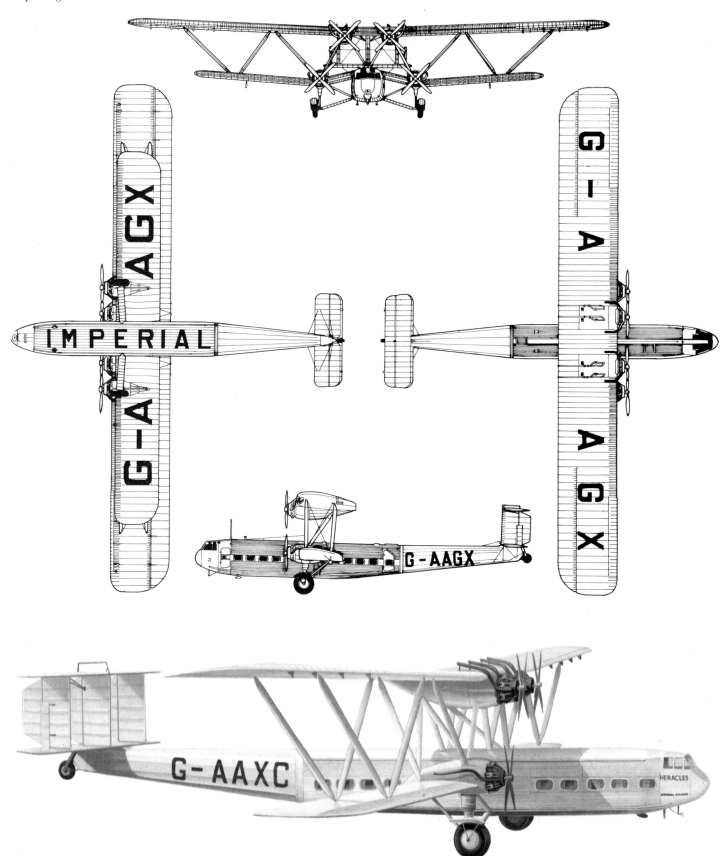

A Junkers G 38 dwarfs an A50 on an airfield in Germany in the early 1930s. The G 38 could carry 34 passengers and a crew of seven

Horatius being lost in 1939, and Hannibal and Horsa in 1940, all in crashes. Hadrian, Hanno and Heracles were all destroyed by gales during 1940. The last aircraft, Helena, was taken apart in August 1941 at the end of a career in which the eight aircraft had flown more than 10 000 000 miles (16 093 000 km), each machine amassing at least 12 000 flying hours. No passenger was ever killed as a result of a civil accident.

By the end of the 1920s, however, the biplane had reached the end of its effective life as an efficient configuration for large land-plane airliners, the success of the HP42/45 owing more to the idiosyncrasies of Imperial Airways' policy than to competition in the world market. However, for short-haul operations with small numbers of passengers the biplane still had a limited future, and for long-haul operations biplane flying boats still offered considerable advantages. The most important of these were the Short Calcutta (15 passengers, three 550-hp [410-kW] Bristol Jupiter IX radials, cruising speed 90 mph [145 km/h], and range 650 miles [1046 km]), the Breguet Br.530 Saïgon version of the Calcutta, the magnificent but unsuccessful 12-engined Dornier Do X, and the Sikorsky S-36 and S-38 series; other notable users of flying boats for commercial purposes were the French, with boats of Breguet and Lioré et Olivier design.

But the aerodynamic way forward had already been shown, initially by the Junkers and Fokker concerns, and then by Lockheed. The ultimate expression of this first phase of monoplane airliner design is perhaps exemplified by the Fokker F XVIII of 1932, of which five were built for KLM. The F XVIII was intended as a 13-seater, passenger accommodation being reduced to six for service in the Far East. Construction was of typical Fokker practice, and the design was based in concept on that of the F VII and F XII tri-motors. Power was provided by three 425-hp (317-kW) Pratt & Whitney Wasps, which gave the type a maximum speed of 149 mph (240 km/h). From this time up to the end of the 1940s, however, Fokker civil aircraft slowly declined in importance, the company being unwilling to drop the high-wing configuration at a time when the adoption of retractable undercarriages called for a low-wing layout to obviate the need for long, heavy and complex folding main legs.

At much the same time, Junkers produced its final two airliners of the classic Junkers configuration with corrugated skinning: the unsuccessful four-engined G 38 and the classic Ju 52 series. The G 38 was the closest the Junkers got to the original 1910 patent for a flying wing commercial aircraft: a giant wing of considerable thickness, spanning 144 ft 4¼ in (44 m) and containing both engines and part of the passenger accommodation, with an abbreviated fuselage projecting forward only slightly in front of the wing, and rearwards to provide a short moment arm for the triple vertical and biplane horizontal tail surfaces. Along the full length of the trailing edge were fitted slotted flaps/ailerons of the type that became standard on all Junkers aircraft, both civil and military, of the 1930s. Powered by four 750-hp (560-kW) Junkers Jumo 204 inlines driving large four-bladed propellers, the G 38 had a maximum speed of 140 mph (225 km/h) and a range of 1180 miles (1900 km). A crew of seven was standard,

and accommodation was provided for up to 34 passengers; up to 6614 lb (3000 kg) of freight could also be carried. Only two examples of the civil G 38 were built, the first flying on 6 November, 1929. The G 38s entered service in 1931 on the Berlin to London route, but the type never proved entirely satisfactory as an airliner. As was standard German practice, the type was also developed as a bomber, the K 51, six of which were built under licence in Japan with the designation Mitsubishi Ki-20.

The evolution of airliner philosophy may be seen in the next major type to appear from the board of the G 38's designer, Ernst Zindel, the Junkers Ju 52 of 1930. Designed as the successor to the F 13, W 33 and W 34, the Ju 52 marked a return to the more conventional type of layout, with a roomy fuselage and slimmer wings, though the typical Junkers slotted flaps/ailerons were retained. Power was provided by a single 725-hp (541-kW) BMW VIIA inline engine, enabling the Ju 52 to carry its three-man crew and a payload of 4409 lb (2000 kg) over a range of 932 miles (1500 km) at a maximum speed of 121 mph (195 km/h). Yet there was clearly room for improvement in the design, and the seventh production Ju 52 was modified to take three engines, initially Pratt & Whitney Hornets, which were just entering licence production in Germany as the BMW 132. Performance and reliability were both improved by a considerable margin, and from the eighth Ju 52 onwards the type was produced as the tri-motor Ju 52/3m, with 660-hp (492-kW) BMW 132A-1 radials in the first production models. The converted model first flew in April 1931, and production models from 1932 onwards. Modifications to accept three engines were relatively small, span being increased by only 9.84 in (25 cm) to 95 ft 11½ in (29.25 m). The performance and payload advantages were great: three crew were still carried, but 17 passengers could be carried at a maximum speed of 180 mph (290 km/h) over a range of 795 miles (1280 km). The Ju 52/3m entered service with Lloyd Aereo Boliviano at the beginning of 1932, and has since enjoyed a career of great versatility and duration, several examples being in full operation at the end of the 1970s. Apart from civil use (including service with British European Airways after World War II), the Ju 52/3m became the transport workhorse of the Luftwaffe before and during World War II, and also served briefly as a bomber. The type was produced in a number of marks with different engines and fittings, many of them for military purposes alone. And despite the fact that the type was technically obsolescent at

JUNKERS JU 52/3m

Type: three-engined medium-range transport
Powerplant: three 600-hp BMW Hornet radials
Accommodation: three or four crew and 15 to 17 passengers

Dimensions: span 95 ft 11½ in (29.2 m); length 92 ft (28 m)
Weights: empty 11 785 lb (5345.5 kg); loaded 20 282 lb (9199 kg)
Performance: maximum speed 180 mph (289.6 km/h); cruising speed 152 mph (244.6 km/h); range 568 miles (914 km)

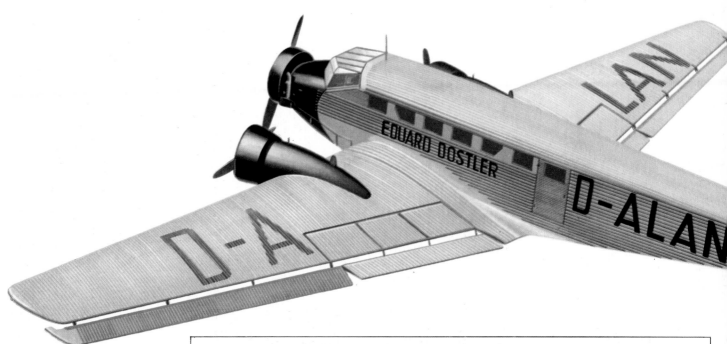

A Lockheed Vega of Continental Airlines: two aircraft could carry the same number of passengers as more expensive twin or tri-motor airliners. Known as Lockheed's 'plywood bullets' the early Vegas established Lockheed as an important aircraft builder. Among the major operators of Vegas were Braniff, Alaska-Washington Airways and Varney Speed Lines. The Vega could also be fitted with floats and in this configuration was used by airlines in Norway, South America and the Caribbean

the beginning of World War II, it remained in production and service throughout.

More advanced in basic concept, however, was the Lockheed Vega, which preceded the Ju 52/3m by some four years. The chief designer of the new Lockheed company was John K Northrop, who together with his superiors was convinced that although Ford and Fokker had a dominating slice of the US airline pie in the late 1920s, their position was by no means unassailable: Ford and Fokker had concentrated on relatively heavy aircraft of tri-motor configuration capable of carrying some 12 passengers. Lockheed saw the weak point in the Ford and Fokker aircraft as being their lack of speed, and Northrop was sure that careful design, with great attention to streamlining and low structural weight, could be combined with a radial engine to produce a small airliner significantly faster than the Ford and Fokker offerings. The result was the beautiful Vega, which entered service with International Airlines on 17 September, 1928. The Vega featured a monocoque plywood fuselage of very fine lines, a well-cowled 425-hp (317-kW) Pratt & Whitney Wasp radial engine, a high-set cantilever wooden wing, and a fixed undercarriage of low drag as a result of its wire-braced single legs and spatted wheels: with a pilot and six passengers the Vega cruised at 135 mph (217 km/h) over a range of 600 miles (966 km), compared with the 4-AT's 100 mph (161 km/h) and 570 miles (917km). Though the seating of the Vega was slightly less than half that of the 4-AT, two Vegas could be operated for the costs of a single 4-AT, the profit lying in the Vegas' 35 mph (56 km/h)

Bottom: The interior of a
Ju 52 of Sabena Airways.
In its military
configuration the Ju 52,
like the Dakota, had seats
facing inwards. In prewar
service the Ju 52 was used
by 30 world airlines.

Below: Lufthansa
technicians service the
three 600-hp BMW
Hornet engines of a
Junkers Ju 52. Prewar Ju
52s were also powered by
French, British and
American radial engines
or even a combination of

engines. Lufthansa had 59
Ju 52s by the autumn of
1939.

greater cruising speed, slightly greater range, and considerably greater operational flexibility. Some 130 Vegas were
built, and soon built up a solid commercial reputation, as
well as acquiring international fame with a number of
record-breaking flights such as the eight-day circumnavi-
gation of the world by Wiley Post and Harold Gatty in the
Vega Winnie Mae between 23 June and 1 July, 1931.

The market for six-seater high-speed monoplanes
opened up by the Vega soon attracted other aircraft: the
two most notable were the Northrop Alpha designed by
John Northrop, and the Boeing 200 Monomail. The
Alpha, introduced by TWA in 1931, was powered by the
same engine as the Vega, but cruised at 140 mph (225
km/h) over a range of 700 miles (1127 km) thanks to even
more careful design of the low-set cantilever wing. The

Boeing 200 Monomail was an altogether larger aircraft,
and had the distinction of being the world's first airliner of
smooth, stressed-skin, cantilever construction. Nearly twice
as heavy as the Lockheed and Northrop aircraft, the
Monomail nevertheless achieved a cruising speed of 135
mph (217 km/h) and a range of 575 miles (925 km) on the
575 hp (429 kW) of its Pratt & Whitney Hornet radial.
Only two Monomails were built, the second being designated Boeing 221A, with accommodation for six passengers and 750 lb (340 kg) of mail, and a retractable
undercarriage. Next appeared the Lockheed Orion, the
world's first commercial aircraft with a maximum speed of
more than 200 mph (322 km/h): powered by a 500-hp
(373-kW) Pratt & Whitney Wasp radial, the Orion carried
six passengers at a cruising speed of 191 mph (307 km/h)
over a range of 750 miles (1207 km), and was introduced
into airline service by Bowen Air Lines in May 1931.
Northrop responded with the Delta, capable of carrying
eight passengers at 175 mph (282 km/h) over ranges of
1550 miles (2494 km) on the power of its 725-hp (541-kW)
Pratt & Whitney Hornet. The Delta was brought into
service by TWA in September 1933. Notable in the
development of these small, single-engined aircraft was the
general trend for the smaller airlines to order such types in
an effort to overcome the financial resources of the larger
airlines by higher speeds and greater ranges. In general,
though, the public did not take to the concept of single-
pilot, single-engine airliners, and the costs of such aircraft
proved generally higher than those of the three-engined
Fords and Fokkers.

The era of the DC3

Airliner design had by the 1930s reached something of a plateau: the airline business, especially in the United States, was thus ripe for the appearance of a new type of airliner combining the technical excellence of the advanced single-engined machines with the safety and operating economics of the tri-motor types, the whole package to offer significant payload and performance advantages in a form acceptable to the public. A move in the right direction was already afoot, as indicated by the appearance of the world's first 'modern' airliner: this was the Boeing 247, which made its initial flight on 8 February, 1933. Among the Boeing aircraft's advanced features were a monocoque fuselage and cantilever monoplane wings of metal construction with stressed metal skinning, two 525-hp (392-kW) Pratt & Whitney Wasp radials in nacelles well forward of the wing leading edge and fitted with drag-reducing NACA cowlings, and a fully retractable under-carriage. The Model 247 used the constructional and building techniques pioneered with the Boeing B-9 mono-plane bomber of 1931, and immediately secured orders for 60 aircraft from Boeing Air Transport, National Air Transport, Pacific Air Transport, and Varney Air Lines, all part of the United Air Lines Group. The Boeing 247 was an immediate success, entering service with United Air Lines on 30 March, 1933. During early operations, the only problem encountered with the Boeing 247 was a certain inadequacy of airfield performance at high-altitude air-ports. The failing was remedied by the introduction of the definitive Boeing 247D model, with Hamilton-Standard variable-pitch propellers: these reduced take-off run by 20%, increased rate of climb by nearly 25%, and boosted cruising speed by 5%. All early Boeing 247s were retrofit-ted with the propellers, and all the 75 Boeing 247s built were finally Model 247Ds. Powered by two 550-hp (410-kW) Pratt & Whitney R-1340-53 Wasp radials, the Boeing 247D carried ten passengers at a cruising speed of 189 mph (304 km/h) over a range of 750 miles (1207 km).

Paradoxically, it was the very success of the Boeing 247 that was largely to blame for its eventual failure to secure more than 75 production orders: with United Air Lines

A Lockheed Model 14 Super Electra, one of the new airliners of the 1930s

A Boeing 247 lands at Burbank airport, California, in 1933. The 247D was an improved version with Hamilton-Standard variable pitch propellers to improve takeoff from high-altitude airfields

taking 70 of the 75, the airline was in a position to dictate the final design of the aircraft, at a time when the Boeing designers were considering the Model 247 as it eventually appeared, or as a larger aircraft powered by a pair of 700-hp (522-kW) Pratt & Whitney Hornets. As it emerged, the Boeing 247 was too small to meet the requirements of many airlines, and even when a giant such as TWA wished to order the type, production was booked so far ahead that the airline had to find another source for its aircraft. Thus TWA turned to other manufacturers on 2 August, 1932 with a request for an advanced tri-motor airliner with seating for 12 passengers in great comfort, plus a cruising speed of 146 mph (235 km/h) or more and a range in excess of 1000 miles (1609 km). Donald W Douglas set his design team to work immediately, and within five days the company's emissaries were on their way to a meeting with TWA representatives with the rough concept for a twin-engined aircraft able to better all TWA's requirements. Tough bargaining followed, largely on the part of Charles Lindbergh, TWA's technical adviser, before a contract was signed on 20 September, 1932 for one aircraft to be designated DC-1 (Douglas Commercial 1), plus an option on 60 more of the type. Thus was set in motion the train of events that was to culminate in the celebrated DC-3, built in larger numbers than any other commercial aircraft before or since.

In concept the DC-1 was a more advanced aircraft than the Boeing 247, with flaps to increase approach angle while reducing speed, a multi-cellular wing structure of the type evolved by John Northrop for strength and long fatigue life, advanced aerodynamics with the aid of Dr W B Oswald of the California Institute of Technology, and effective soundproofing for the 12 passengers. Work on the DC-1 advanced quite quickly, the most difficult point being the selection of a powerplant, both Pratt & Whitney and Wright pressing the merits of their engines. At the end of June 1933 the DC-1 was finally ready, powered by a pair

Above: The interior of a Boeing 247D; the 247D appeared in the mid 1930s. The crew consisted of two with a stewardess to look after the ten passengers

CURTISS T-32 CONDOR

Type: twin-engined medium-range transport
Powerplant: two 700-hp Wright Cyclones
Accommodation: two crew and 15 passengers
Dimensions: span 82 ft (25 m); length 49 ft 1 in (14.9 m)
Weights: loaded 16 800 lb (7620.3 kg); empty 11 235 lb (5084.8 kg)
Performance: maximum speed 170 mph (273.5 km/h); cruising speed 150 mph (241 km/h)

A Douglas DC-2. Capable of
carrying 14 passengers with a
crew of two, the DC-2 had a
range of 1060 miles (1705.8 km)

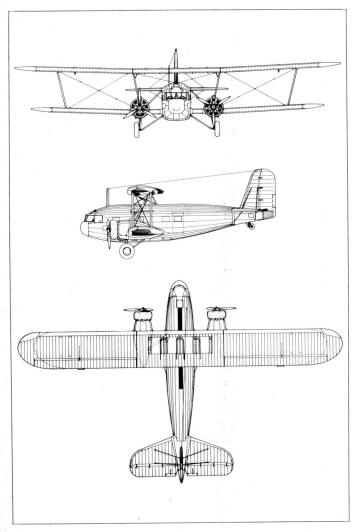

of Wright R-1820-F radials. The first flight was made on 1
July, and the aircraft was handed over to TWA in
December 1933, to the full satisfaction of the customer.
Certain improvements were called for, however, and this
resulted in the DC-2, limiting DC-1 production to the
single aircraft. The main difference between the DC-1 and
-2 was the increases of passenger capacity to 14 in the later
aircraft by the stretching of the fuselage by 24 in (60.96
cm), and the use of the more powerful Wright R-1820-F3
radials.

The DC-2 entered service on 18 May, 1934, and made
even the Boeing 247 appear obsolete. Although the Boeing
247D was more a match for the DC-2 in performance, the
Boeing aircraft had the unfortunate feature of the main
spar cutting the passenger cabin neatly into two, a factor
unappreciated by customers; and the split flaps of the DC-
2 proved very popular with airlines, again to the detriment
of the Boeing 247 and 247D. However, United Air Lines
were committed to the Boeing 247, and could not join the
other major airlines rushing to buy the new world leader in
airliner design and capability. The success of the DC-2 led
to the immediate retirement of the Fokker and Ford tri-
motors by the major airlines, the only major survivor of the
1920s being the Curtiss Condor, the sleeper version of
which, with accommodation for 14 and power provided by
a pair of 700-hp (522-kW) Wright R-1820-F Cyclones, had
entered service with American Airlines only in May 1934.
This biplane did not long survive the arrival of the DC-2,
however, despite the range limitations of the latter, which
meant that the Condor 32 was theoretically better suited
for long-range sleeper flights. The DC-2 had a cruising
speed of 190 mph (306 km/h) and a normal range of 1000
miles (1609 km), though stages of more than 500 miles
(805 km) were rarely flown. Production of the DC-2
totalled 220 aircraft.

By any standard the DC-2 was an assured success, but yet
greater things were to come, largely as the result of an

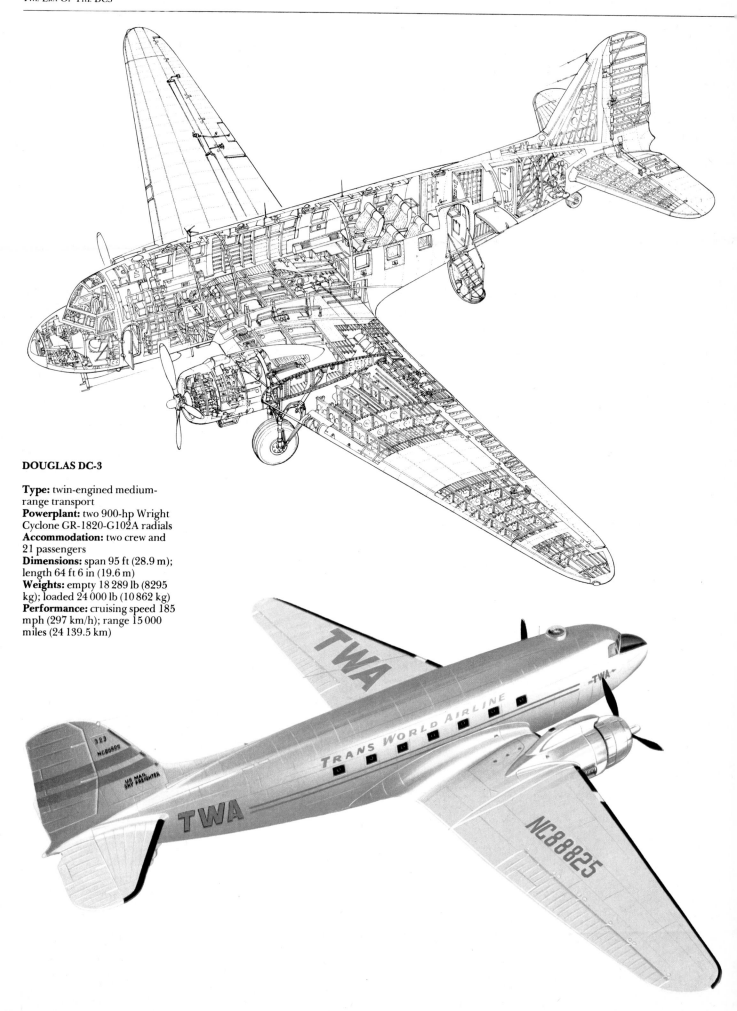

DOUGLAS DC-3

Type: twin-engined medium-range transport
Powerplant: two 900-hp Wright Cyclone GR-1820-G102A radials
Accommodation: two crew and 21 passengers
Dimensions: span 95 ft (28.9 m); length 64 ft 6 in (19.6 m)
Weights: empty 18 289 lb (8295 kg); loaded 24 000 lb (10 862 kg)
Performance: cruising speed 185 mph (297 km/h); range 15 000 miles (24 139.5 km)

initiative from American Airlines. Distressed by the failure of their Condor 32 sleeper series, American Airlines approached Douglas with a suggestion for an enlarged version of the DC-2, with a wider fuselage to accommodate sleeper berths. Douglas, already committed to the hilt with production of the DC-2 for European as well as US orders, was at first reluctant, finally being swayed by American Airlines' intention to buy 20 of the new type.

Thus there flew for the first time on 17 December, 1935 the original DST (Douglas Sleeper Transport): this was basically the DC-2 with a different fuselage, widened by 26 in (66.04 cm) and lengthened by 30¼ in (76.84 cm) to accommodate 14 sleeper berths. At the same time the contours of the fuselage were altered, with rounded sides replacing the straight sides of the DC-2, and the nose acquiring different contours as a result of the relocation of the landing lights to the wing leading edges. Other alterations included strengthened and lengthened wings, with a span of 95 ft (28.96 m) compared with the DC-2's 85 ft (25.9 m), extra fuel tankage and enlarged tail surfaces. The potential of the aircraft in its latest form was recognized by American Airlines with a confirmed order for eight DSTs and 12 DC-3s, and the dayplane version with seating for 21 passengers was designated. The DST entered service, in fact as a dayplane, on 25 June, 1936, and so started the era of the DC-3 proper, thanks to the efforts of American Airlines and the risk-taking willingness of Douglas.

Almost immediately the DC-3 rendered even the DC-2 obsolete: powered by two Wright R-1820-G2 Cyclones or Pratt & Whitney R-1830 Wasps, the DC-3 had almost the same performance as the DC-2, but aerodynamic improvements combined with extra seating meant that the DC-3 could carry 50% more payload than its predecessor for only 10% greater operating costs. The success of the DC-3 was signalled by an enormous demand for the type, and even the most committed Boeing 247 user, United Air Lines, was forced to buy the new type. It is impossible to overemphasize the importance of the DC-3 in world aviation history. A few facts thus speak for themselves: production of the DC-3 and all its divers variants totalled no less than 10654 aircraft between 1935 and 1947 by Douglas, with a further 485 being built in Japan under licence by Showa and Nakajima as the L2D, and about 2000 in the USSR under licence by Lisunov as the Li-2 'Cab', for a grand total of at least 13139; by the time of Japan's attack on Pearl Harbor in December 1941, US airline fleets were made up largely of DC-3s, some 260 of the type being in service out of a total strength of 322; and in 1939 some 90% of the world's airline passenger traffic was carried in DC-3s.

As it had in the late 1920s, Lockheed now felt that its undoubted technical expertise was capable of capturing for the company some of the airlines' seemingly insatiable demand for the latest all-metal airliners of advanced aerodynamic and structural concept. Unable to compete with Douglas in terms of volume production, Lockheed thus turned again to the small airliner able to outfly the DC-3: the result was the superb Lockeed L.10 Electra, which entered service on 11 August, 1934 with Northwest Airlines. Powered by two 450-hp (336-kW) Pratt & Whit-

ney R-985-13 radials, the Electra carried 12 passengers at a cruising speed of 185 mph (298 km/h) over a range of 500 miles (805 km/h), some 20 mph (32 km/h) better than could be achieved by the DC-3 over the same stage length when the latter entered service some 22 months later. The slightly smaller and less powerful Lockheed L.12 carried eight passengers over the same distance at a cruising speed of 212 mph (341 km/h), while the Lockheed L.14 could carry 12 passengers over a range of 2160 miles (3476 km) at a cruising speed of 255 mph (410 km/h) on the power of its two 1000-hp (746-kW) Wright GR-1820-G205A radials after its introduction by Northwest Airlines in September, 1937, 15 months after the DC-3's airline debut. The production of the three Lockheed types was 148, 114 and 112 respectively.

The appearance of the Boeing 247, the Douglas DC-3 and the Lockheed L.10 Electra had transformed the shape of airliners totally, and at last brought into airline operating economics the chance of considerable profits by the carriage of passengers alone, without the supplementary carriage of air mail. The important factors of the three US aircraft, compared with their predecessors, were as follows: low-wing monoplane configuration with all-metal stressed-skin construction and smooth finish; all-metal monocoque fuselage construction; two wing-mounted engines of considerable power, with superchargers and low-drag cowlings; variable-pitch propellers; retractable

The Electra in a travel brochure setting. Electras were widely used before the war and five were operated by the Polish airline LOT. Though they escaped to Bucharest in 1939 they were later captured and used by the Luftwaffe. Electras are still in service in smaller airlines

Below: The CW-20 and later its
more powerful adaptation the
C-45, known as the Commando,
were built at the beginning of the
war in Europe and later as
military transports. In 1945
surplus aircraft made up part of
the world's emergent peacetime
airlines

CURTISS WRIGHT CW-20

Type: twin-engined medium-
range transport
Powerplant: two 17 000-hp
Wright Double Row Cyclone
586-C 14-BA2 radials
Accommodation: two crew and
36 passengers
Dimensions: span 108 ft (32.9
m); length 75 ft (22.86 m)
Weights: empty 29 500 lb (13 380
kg); loaded 45 000 lb (20 411 kg)
Performance: maximum speed
243 mph (391 km/h); cruising
speed 195 mph (313.8 km/h)

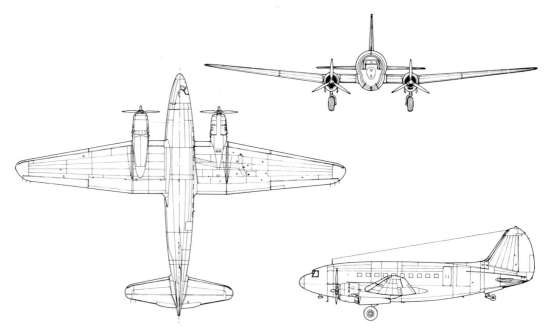

CITY OF CARDIFF

G-ABCI

DE HAVILLAND DH 84
DRAGON

Type: twin-engined short-range
transport
Powerplant: two 130-hp de
Havilland Gipsy Major
Accommodation: two crew and
six passengers
Dimensions: span 47 ft 4 in (14.4
m); length 34 ft 6 in (10.5 m)
Weights: empty 2300 lb (1043
kg); loaded 4200 lb (1905 kg)
Performance: maximum speed
128 mph (205 km/h); cruising
speed 109 mph (175 km/h);
range 460 miles (738.9 km)

undercarriages; and trailing edge flaps to lower landing speed, except on the Boeing 247. Another important feature, used only on the Boeing 247, was the provision of inflatable de-icing 'boots' to allow safer operation in poor weather conditions.

Such was the dominance of the Douglas DC-3 that the European efforts at the same type of airliner paled into virtual obscurity by comparison, and no other US twin-engined airliner entered service until after the end of the decade. Even then there were only two direct competitors for the DC-3, in the form of the Curtiss CW-20, generally known by the designation of its military counterpart, the C-46 Commando, and the Lockheed L.18 Lodestar.

The CW-20 resulted from a 1936 requirement for a two-engined, pressurized airliner with double the payload of the DC-3. With accommodation for 36 passengers, the CW-20 first flew in March, 1940, when it was clear that the civil applications for the type would be limited as a result of the war already involving much of Europe and likely to spread. Powered by a pair of 2400-hp (1790-kW) Pratt & Whitney R-2800-CB16 radials, the CW-20 featured a capacious fuselage which could carry up to 40 passengers when the pressurization system was removed, with a cruising speed of 227 mph (365 km/h) over a range of 2300 miles (3701 km). The type was thus ideally suited to the carriage of troops or freight over moderately long ranges, and to this end the 3180 C-46s built for civil and military operation played an important part in World War II, many ex-military aircraft being sold to civil operators at the end of hostilities. The C-46 entered service with the Military Transport Division of Eastern Air Lines on 1 October, 1942. The Lockheed L.18 Lodestar preceded the C-46 into service, Mid-Continent Airlines starting the first Lodestar service in March 1940. The airliner, capable of carrying 17 passengers, was the ultimate expression of the Lockheed limited-payload but high-speed philosophy, and embodied all the lessons learned with the other twin-engined Lockheed civil types. Of great aerodynamic cleanliness, and featuring all the advanced high-lift devices of the day, the Lodestar cruised at 229 mph (369 km/h) over a range of 1800 miles (2897 km) on the power of two 900-hp (671-kW) Wright GR-1820-G107A radials. And as the L.14 had been developed into the military A-28, A-29 and Hudson maritime patrol bombers and reconnaissance aircraft, the L.18 was developed into the PV-1 Ventura and then the PV-2 Harpoon patrol bombers.

The difference between the European and US design philosophies at the beginning of the 1930s is readily apparent with even the most careless glance at two near-contemporary designs, the Junkers Ju 52/3m and the Boeing 247. Yet the British were even further removed from the US concept, as shown by the introduction at about the same time of the Handley Page HP42/45 series, and two superb if technically obsolescent biplanes, the de Havilland DH84 Dragon in 1932, and the DH89 Dragon Rapide in 1934.

The DH84 was the result of the success enjoyed by the DH83 Fox Moth (four passengers and one 145-hp [108-kW] de Havilland Gipsy Major 1C inline engine) in service as a 'feederliner' with Hillmans Airways and other operators at the beginning of the decade. Edward Hillman

therefore asked de Havilland for a twin-engined version with greater range. The result of this and other requests was the DH84, which first flew on 24 November, 1932 and entered service in December 1932. But whereas the Fox Moth had been a monoplane, for the DH84 the designers reverted to the well-proved biplane formula. The new machine was given a very clean look, though, despite the wooden construction: the nose had a very clean entry, with the extensively glazed cockpit right in the nose and the accommodation for the six passengers immediately behind it; the two 130-hp (97-kW) de Havilland Gipsy Major inline engines were neatly installed in nacelles in the lower wing leading edge, with the carefully streamlined and spatted mainwheels under them. Cost and design effort were saved by the use of mainplanes from the DH60G Gipsy Moth lightplane for the outer wing panels. With six passengers and 270 lb (122.5 kg) of luggage, the Dragon cruised at 109 mph (175 km/h) and had a range of 460 miles (740 km), though these figures were raised to 114 mph (183 km/h) and 545 miles (877 km) in the Dragon with faired undercarriage struts. Total production ran to 115 aircraft.

Late in 1933 de Havilland began work on a more advanced model of the Dragon, with greater speed and more passenger comfort. The result was the beautiful DH89 Dragon Rapide biplane, which had the same general lines as the DH84 Dragon, but was more akin in concept and design to the DH86 four-engined airliner (ten seats, four 200-hp [149-kW] de Havilland Gipsy Six Series I inline engines, cruising speed of 142 mph [229 km/h], and range of 760 miles [1223 km] in the DH86A). The fuselage had very fine lines, the wings were finely tapered, the engines were located in large but well-streamlined nacelles, and the single mainwheels were located in 'trousers' under the nacelles. The first example flew on 17 April, 1934, and this example was followed by another 727 of the type. Powered by two 200-hp (149-kW) de Havilland Gipsy Six or de Havilland Gipsy Queen inline engines, the DH89 had a maximum speed of 157 mph (253 km/h), a cruising speed of 132 mph (212 km/h) and a range with eight passengers of 578 miles (930 km).

Far more advanced in concept was the Bristol 142, which first flew on 12 April, 1935. The basic design for a twin-engined passenger aircraft, powered by Bristol Aquila I radials, was already roughed out when the Douglas DC-1 first flew in the USA: this occasioned a certain amount of nationalistic pride in the UK, and Lord Rothermere, owner of the *Daily Mail*, responded by ordering a version of this Bristol 135 with performance superior to that of the DC-1. This appeared as the Bristol 142, capable of carrying four passengers in addition to its crew of two. Powered by two 650-hp (485-kW) Bristol Mercury VIS2 radials, the Type 142 had a top speed of 307 mph (490 km/h) and a range of 1000 miles (1609 km). The performance of the aircraft was sparkling (top speed being 50 mph [80 km/h] more than that of the latest Gloster Gladiator fighter), but despite its advanced concept, with all the latest technical features for the first time on a British airliner, the Type 142 was not an economic prospect as a commercial aircraft, and its main distinction lies in the fact that it was the immediate progenitor of the Bristol Blenheim light bomber.

In the same sort of way, the Boeing 247 also provided the stimulus for two German airliners, the Dornier Do 17 and the Junkers Ju 86. The origins of the Do 17 lay in a Deutsche Lufthansa requirement for a very fast mailplane to operate on European routes, with the additional capacity to carry six passengers. By the end of 1934 the first three prototypes had flown, demonstrating excellent performance with their sleek lines, the latter marred only by the somewhat angular nacelles for the two 660-hp (492-kW) BMW VI inline engines. Maximum speed was 270 mph (435 km/h) and cruising speed 242 mph (390 km/h), but the whole concept was rendered impractical as a commercial aircraft by the passenger accommodation: two people in a tiny cabin aft of the flight deck, and four people in another tiny cabin aft of the wing, both being accessible only to persons of some gymnastic ability. Early in 1935 it was decided to abandon the type, but then Flugkapitän Untucht, Deutsche Lufthansa's liaison officer with the Luftwaffe, visited Dornier and was so impressed with the performance of the Do 17 that he suggested the type's development as a *Schnellbomber* (fast bomber), as which the Do 17 'Flying Pencil' has mainly gone down in history.

The Junkers Ju 86 was a totally more realistic concept as an airliner, though it had in fact been designed to a dual requirement that called for the type to be used with minimal changes as a commercial aircraft but also as a bomber. The specification was issued in early 1934 to Junkers and Heinkel: in response Junkers tendered the Ju 86, Heinkel the He 111, the former owing much to the single-engined Ju 60 (six passengers, one 525-hp [392-kW] BMW-built Hornet, maximum speed 174 mph [280 km/h]) and basically similar Ju 160 (six passengers, one 660-hp [492-kW] BMW 132E radial, maximum speed 208 mph [335 km/h], range 684 miles [1100 km]), the latter to the single-engined He 70 *Blitz* (four passengers, one 750-hp [560-kW] BMW VI 7,3Z inline, maximum speed 208 mph

[335 km/h], range 621 miles [1000 km]). Both the Ju 70 and the He 70 were intended as fast mailplanes with accommodation for a few passengers, but the He 70 is especially significant as the first 'modern' airliner produced by the European aircraft industry in the 1930s, the twin brothers Walter and Siegfried Günter designing a highly efficient low-wing monoplane with elliptical wings, an oval monocoque fuselage of dural, a well-cowled engine and retractable undercarriage, the result being an aircraft with very pleasing yet at the same time menacing lines. The He 70 was also developed as a fast reconnaissance and bomber aircraft.

The first Ju 86 made its maiden flight on 4 November, 1934, having been completed in only five months. A certain measure of the typical Junkers angularity was still there in the design, as were the slotted flaps/ailerons, but construction was in the smooth metal pioneered by Junkers with the Ju 60 and Ju 160. Power was to be provided by two Junkers Jumo 205 diesel engines, which were heavier than contemporary petrol engines of the same power, but were smaller in frontal area and decidedly superior in fuel consumption. The bomber and airliner models were all but identical, the bomber's gun positions being deleted in the civil model, and the vertical bomb cells replaced by individual seating for ten passengers, each with a window, in a fuselage only 57 in (1.45 m) wide. In the event, only 13 Junkers Ju 86 airliners for Deutsche Lufthansa were built, remaining in service from 1936 to 1940. Powered by 600-hp (448-kW) Jumo 205C diesels, the typical Ju 86B seated ten passengers in addition to the crew of three, had a maximum speed of 193 mph (310 km/h), and could fly 1553 miles (2500 km) at a cruising speed of 174 mph (280 km/h).

The Heinkel He 111 was also designed to the same dual requirement as the Ju 86, and was intended in its civil guise as a ten-seat airliner to build up Germany's reputation for

Left: A de Havilland DH84
Dragon, one of the 115 built
at Stag Lane and Hatfield.
The first flight was in November
1932 and the Dragon was
eventually to be sold all over
the world. It was ideal for small
internal airlines

Below: A de Havilland DH 89
banks over an airfield prior to
landing. The Dragon Rapide first
flew in 1934 and was still in
widespread use in the 1950s. It
was not until the Britten-Norman
Islander was introduced that it
had any real rivals

fast and regular commercial services within Europe.
Designed by Walter and Siegfried Günter, the He 111
displayed typical Heinkel design flair with its sweeping,
elegant lines and elliptical wing planform. Appearing in
January 1936, however, the He 111 also displayed severe
limitations in the passenger role, for reasons largely the
same as the Do 17: the passenger accommodation was
divided and cramped, with four people accommodated in a
forward cabin between the main spars, and the other six in
a small compartment aft of the wing rear spar. Only six He
111C and four He 111G commercial versions were built, as
by the end of 1936 Deutsche Lufthansa had seen that the
type would have hopeless operating economics. Powered
by two 660-hp (492-kW) BMW VIU inline engines, the He-
111C-0 carried ten passengers, had a maximum speed of
214 mph (345 km/h), and could fly 932 miles (1500 km) at
a cruising speed of 186 mph (300 km/h). Like the Do 17,
the He 111 was to find its niche in history as one of the
Luftwaffe's main bombers throughout World War II.

During the late 1920s and early 1930s, the Italian
aircraft industry also produced a number of interesting tri-
motor airliners, most of them of Caproni or Savoia-
Marchetti origin: Caproni may be regarded as the Italian
equivalent of Fokker, so far as design was concerned, for
its aircraft were generally of the high-wing monoplane
type, though built of metal and braced; Savoia-Marchetti,
on the other hand, may be seen as the Italian counterpart
of Junkers, favouring low-wing cantilever monoplanes,
though the finish was smooth rather than corrugated. The
Savoia-Marchetti airliners reached their peak with the
SM.73, a clean tri-motor airliner of thoroughbred lines,
powered by three radial engines in well-cowled nacelles,
and fitted with a low-drag undercarriage with spatted
wheels. The SM.73 finally led to the SM.81 bomber and
transport for the Regia Aeronautica, and the SM.81 in turn
gave birth to the SM.79. This last was basically a cleaned-up

SM.81 fitted with a retractable undercarriage, intended at
first for the 1934 'MacRobertson' air race from England to
Australia. In the event the type was too late for the race,
but it was then developed as an airliner with a payload of
2515 lb (1140 kg), and finally into Italy's best bomber of
World War II.

After a hesitant start into the field of civil aviation in the
1920s, the USSR began to make considerable strides in the
1930s, despite the country's major preoccupation with
military hardware in the technical sciences and in production facilities. One of the great figures in aviation history,
Andrei Tupolev, had already entered the scene with
aircraft such as the ANT-9 of 1929, which could carry
eight passengers. It was a high-wing monoplane of metal
construction but limited aerodynamic efficiency, powered
by three 230-hp (172-kW) Gnome-Rhône Titan or 300-hp
(224-kW) M-26 radials. In 1932 there appeared a twin-
engined version, the ANT-9/M-17 powered by 680-hp
(507-kW) M-17 engines. Maximum speed of the ANT-9
was 115 mph (185 km/h), and that of the ANT-9/M-17 147
mph (237 km/h). The ANT-14 of 1931 was basically an
enlarged version of the ANT-9, with five 480-hp (358-kW)
M-22 radials, and intended for long-haul routes. Spanning
132 ft 6 in (40.39 m), the ANT-14 generally carried a crew
of six and 36 passengers, but a high-density accommodation for 65 could be arranged. Even larger was the ANT-20
'Maxim Gorki' of 1934. Powered by eight 900-hp (671-kW)
AM-34RN inline engines (six in the wings, and the last two
in a strut-mounted nacelle above the fuselage driving a
tractor and a pusher propeller), the ANT-20 was at the
time the world's largest aircraft, spanning 206 ft 8 in (63
m): with a passenger capacity of up to 80, the ANT-20 had
a top speed of 137 mph (220 km/h). Like all previous
Tupolev aircraft, the constructional method and design
philosophy (apart from size) was closely akin to that of
Junkers, which had established production facilities in the
USSR during the early 1920s. The ANT-20 was derived
from the ANT-6 bomber, and the sole example was
destroyed in an aerial collision in 1935. More importantly,
however, Tupolev followed the ANT-20 with the ANT-
20bis of 1935, the eight engines of the earlier type being
replaced by six 1100-hp (821-kW) M-100 inline engines.
Passenger accommodation for 64 was provided, and 16 of
the type were built. Maximum speed was 171 mph (275
km/h).

But Tupolev's most important civil aircraft to appear
before World War II was the ANT-35 of 1935. This
was the first 'modern' Soviet airliner, with smooth metal
finish and sleek lines. Powered by a pair of 850-hp
(634-kW) M-85 radials, the ANT-35 carried a crew of two
and ten passengers at a maximum speed of 268 mph (432
km/h), and entered service in 1937. Other Soviet civil types
were produced in the 1930s, but these were mostly of the
smaller, single-engined type such as the Kalinin K-5 of
1931: powered by a 480-hp (358-kW) M-22 radial, the K-5
featured a braced high-set wing of elliptical planform.
Another interesting type of the era was the ChAI-1 of
1932: this was a low-wing cantilever monoplane with a
retractable undercarriage, and could carry six passengers
at 199 mph (320 km/h) on the 480 hp (358 kW) of its
Townend-ringed M-22 radial.

The four-engined airliner

Although four-engined civil aircraft had appeared as early as 1913, and been developed into practical form with both biplane and monoplane configurations by a number of European designers in the late 1920s and early 1930s, the definitive period for the design of 'modern' four-engined airliners only arrived in the late 1930s: with two- and three-engined airliners meeting the need for short- and medium-haul operations, the airlines astutely realized that the next step in passenger services would be a reduction in journey times for long-range services, and a consequent improvement in passenger comfort, by the increase in stage lengths. The latest aerodynamic and structural concepts could be combined, therefore, to produce large passenger aircraft with long ranges: four engines would ensure great reliability as well as adequate reserves of power, structural and aerodynamic improvements would ensure safety and operating economy, and the size of the aircraft envisaged would provide high seating capacity as well as room for freight, mail and luggage, as well as extra facilities such as a galley, extra lavatories, more flight attendants and other ancillary equipment essential to the well-being of the passengers on long flights. It was anticipated that the aircraft of this new generation would also be more complex than those of the current generation with provision of considerably superior instrumentation such as artificial horizons, directional gyros and radio direction-finding equipment, as well as power-boosted controls, retractable tricycle undercarriages, more efficient high-lift devices, efficient cabin pressurization, de-icing equipment, and more sophisticated methods of getting the best performance out of the increasingly reliable and economical aero engines. In this last category fell variable-pitch propellers, constant-speed propellers, automatic supercharging and semi-automatic cooling systems.

The first of the new four-engined airliners was the Douglas DC-4E, whose origins lay in 1935 discussions between Douglas and United Air Lines for an airliner with twice the capacity of the DC-3, which had not yet flown. However, neither Douglas nor United had the capital to risk on such a venture, and it was not until March 1936 that

The Stratoliner gave travellers comfort and speed in the late '40s

BOEING 307 STRATOLINER

Type: four-engined long-range transport
Powerplant: four 1100-hp Wright R-1320-G201A radials
Accommodation: five crew and 33 passengers
Dimensions: span 107 ft 3 in (32.6 m); length 74 ft 4 in (22.5 m)
Weights: gross 42 000 lb (19 050.7 kg)
Performance: maximum speed 246 mph (395.8 km/h); cruising speed 200 mph (321 km/h); range 1200 miles (1931 km)

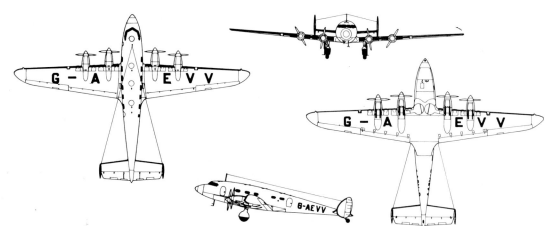

DE HAVILLAND DH 91 ALBATROS

Type: four-engined long-range transport
Powerplant: four 525-hp de Havilland Gipsy Twelve series 1
Accommodation: four crew and 22 passengers
Dimensions: span 105 ft (32 m); length 71 ft 6 in (21.7 m)
Weights: empty 21 230 lb (9629 kg); loaded (passengers) 29 500 lb (13 380 kg); (mail) 32 500 lb (14 741 kg)
Performance: maximum speed 225 mph (362 km/h); cruising speed 210 mph (337 km/h); range 3300 miles (5310 km)

American, Eastern, Pan American, TWA and United Airlines agreed each to contribute $100 000 to the development of the DC-4, as the project was at first entitled: seating was to be for 42 passengers in double rows on each side of a central aisle, with an alternative layout for 30 sleeper berths; power was to be provided by four 1450-hp (1082-kW) Pratt & Whitney R2180-S1A1-G radials; slotted flaps were to be fitted; the undercarriage was to be of the tricycle type, the first time that such gear had been envisaged for an aircraft of this size; controls were to be power-boosted; and production aircraft were to be fully pressurized, enabling the aircraft to cruise at high altitude, thereby taking full advantage of engine fuel economy and superior atmospheric conditions, without any discomfort for the passengers. With hindsight it is possible to see that the Douglas designers had set themselves too formidable a task, with too many advanced features in an aircraft of such novelty and size. The fact that the airlines were also worried by the complexity of the project is reflected in the decision of Pan American and TWA to drop out of the risk-sharing financial agreement during the summer of 1936. The aircraft was nonetheless completed in May 1938, and first flew on 7 June of the same year. Numerous problems were encountered with the aircraft's systems, and

it was soon clear that the operating costs of the type would be prohibitively expensive. The DC-4E was handed over to United Air Lines in May 1939, and started a limited programme of development services on 1 June, 1939. By this time passenger capacity had been increased to 52, but the type still failed to meet United's requirements, and was sold to Greater Japan Air Lines late in 1939. This was a front for the purchase of the type for the Japanese navy: it was reported that the DC-4E had crashed into Tokyo Bay, but in fact it had been taken apart by Nakajima as part of the programme to develop the imperial navy's Nakajima G5N1 *Shinzan* heavy bomber. The DC-4E had a maximum speed of 245 mph (394 km/h), a cruising speed of 200 mph (322 km/h) and a range of 2200 miles (3540 km).

Far more important, though, was the Boeing 307 Stratoliner, which entered service with TWA on 8 July, 1940. A less ambitious project than the Douglas DC-4E, the Stratoliner resulted from a decision in 1936 by Pan American and TWA to help finance a four-engined airliner other than the Douglas aircraft. Boeing was thus well-placed to offer an airliner derived in part from the company's celebrated B-17 Flying Fortress heavy bomber, which was already in service with the US Army Air Corps. The same type of wing and tail surfaces were employed in

SHORT S23 EMPIRE FLYING BOAT

Type: four-engined long-range flying boat
Powerplant: four 1010-hp Bristol Pegasus XC
Accommodation: five crew with 24 day passengers or 16 night berths
Dimensions: span 114 ft (34.7 m); length 88 ft (26.8 m)
Weights: empty 23 500 lb (10 659 kg); loaded 40 500 lb (18 370 kg)
Performance: maximum speed 200 mph (321.8 km/h); cruising speed 165 mph (265.5 km/h); range 760 miles (1223 km)

the Stratoliner, but the fuselage featured a modicum of pressurization, and this allowed the Stratoliner to cruise at 14 000 ft (4265 m), somewhat higher than that possible with the unpressurized DC-3, and just about high enough to avoid some 90% of the weather problems affecting operation at lower altitude. The Stratoliner was the first civil airliner to feature pressurization, and proved immediately successful. Used for flights across the United States, the Boeing 307 had only a short career, for the ten aircraft built were all commandeered for transatlantic operations from 24 December, 1941. All survived the war and were returned to civil operations afterwards. Powered by four 1100-hp (821-kW) Wright R-1320-G201A radials, the Boeing 307 carried 33 passengers at a cruising speed of 200 mph (321 km/h) over a range of 1200 miles (1931 km). An aircraft of less complexity and ambition than the DC-4E, the Boeing 307 proved successful in its own right, but also proved the validity of pressurized four-engined airliners for commercial operations. Essentially an interim type with its limited payload, performance, tailwheel-type undercarriage and low pressurization differential, the Boeing 307 showed what the future could expect, and its promise was more than fulfilled by the great success of the postwar Boeing 377 Stratocruiser.

Towards the end of the 1930s, the renascent European aircraft industry had also come to the conclusion that the future of long-range commercial aviation lay with high-performance four-engined land-planes, although the European conviction did not extend as far as pressurization at this time. The three most important types to the new formula were the German Focke-Wulf Fw 200 Condor, and the British Armstrong Whitworth AW.27 Ensign and de Havilland DH91 Albatros.

The Fw 200 stemmed from discussions between Focke-Wulf's chief designer, Kurt Tank, and Deutsche Lufthansa in 1936 on the possibility of a transatlantic airliner. Tank expressed the view that such a machine was possible, but that it would have to be four-engined, and that wings of higher aspect ratio than was normal would have to be used. Deutsche Lufthansa agreed to sponsor the development of such a machine, and the first Fw 200 flew on 27 July, 1937, just over one year after the signature of the contract. Few problems were encountered with the prototype, which was powered by four 875-hp (653-kW) Pratt & Whitney Hornet S1E-G radials. Operations with Danish and Brazilian companies, as well as with Deutsche Lufthansa, got under way in July 1938 and the succeeding months. Delivery of the new type was slow, however, largely as a result of the

A de Havilland DH 91 Albatros
arrives at Croydon Airport in
1939. The Albatros survived
until 1944 when crashes and lack
of spares led to the retirement of
the last two of the seven original
aircraft

The Armstrong Whitworth
Atalanta was powered by four
Bristol Siddeley Serval III
engines which had formerly been
called Double Mongoose engines

Right: The Short L17 was
powered by four 595 hp Bristol
Jupiter XFBM radials. It could
carry 39 passengers but only two
were built in the mid 1930s

experimental work being carried out with a number of
early models. In its definitive Fw 200B form, the Condor
was powered by four 845-hp (630-kW) BMW 132Dc
radials, which enabled the type to carry a crew of four and
26 passengers at a maximum speed of 261 mph (420
km/h), and over a range of 1243 miles (2000 km) at a
cruising speed of 242 mph (390 km/h). Clearly the range of
the laden passenger model was still less than that required
for transatlantic operations, but considerable improvements were expected in later models with improved
engines. At this stage, however, military requirements
intervened, and the Fw 200 was turned into a useful, if not
perfect, maritime reconnaissance aircraft, largely as a
result of Japanese requirements. It is as such, accordingly,
that the Fw 200 is best remembered today, as are many
other German types of the time. Focke-Wulf was also
working on an improved model, it should be noted: the Fw
300 was to have a crew of five, and carry 40 passengers on
the power of its four 1950-hp (1455-kW) Daimler-Benz
DB603 inlines; with these engines maximum speed was
estimated at 327 mph (527 km/h), cruising speed 267 mph
(430 km/h) and range 5095 miles (8200 km).

The other German four-engined airliner of the period
was the Junkers Ju 90, designed by Ernst Zindel and based
largely on the abortive Ju 89 strategic bomber. The first
example flew on 28 August, 1937, but only a few production aircraft were ever delivered to Deutsche Lufthansa,
considerable effort then being expended on the development of the type as the Ju 290 maritime reconnaissance
bomber and transport. The Ju 90B civil airliner was
powered by four 750-hp (560-kW) BMW 132H radials,
and was distinctly underpowered: crew comprised four
men, and up to 40 passengers could be carried at a
maximum speed of 192 mph (310 km/h), though the best
range of 1243 miles (2000 km) was achieved at a cruising
speed of 180 mph (290 km/h).

Like these two German aircraft, the Armstrong Whitworth Ensign and de Havilland Albatros were more
European expressions of the US DC-3 design philosophy
upgraded to four-engined status, than true examples of
what the US had achieved with the Boeing 307, and had
almost achieved with the Douglas DC-4E. The AW.27
Ensign was intended, as always with aircraft for Imperial
Airways, as a combined mail- and passenger-carrier, and
began life in response to a 1934 requirement for a fast
mailplane for service on the routes to South Africa and
Australia. Most of Imperial Airways' requirement was to be
met by a large fleet of Short Empire-class flying boats (the
C and G classes), but for the European and Far East routes
a land-plane was required, able to carry passengers as well
as mail. Armstrong Whitworth, whose AW.XV Atalanta
four-engined airliner had entered service with Imperial
Airways in 1932, agreed to tender to the requirement.
(The Atalanta had been a clean cantilever monoplane with
high set wings, with the unusual feature of mainwheels
attached to the bottom of the fuselage by short legs; only
eight had been built, powered by four 340-hp [254-kW]
Armstrong Siddeley Serval III radials, and these could
each carry 2240 lb [1016 kg] of mail and nine passengers,
or 17 passengers and no mail, at a cruising speed of 118
mph [190km/h] over a range of 640 miles [1030 km]. In
service the Atalanta supplemented the Handley Page
HP42/45 series and the ungainly Short Scylla four-engined
biplane. The Scylla was a land-plane derivative of the Short
Kent flying boat, developed in 1933 when Imperial Airways could not buy more HP42s. Using the same wings, tail
and powerplant as the Kent, the two Scyllas could carry 38
passengers at a maximum speed of 137 mph [220 km/h].)

At the insistence of Imperial Airways, Armstrong Whitworth were forced to adopt a four-engined high-wing
monoplane layout, and so the AW.27 Ensign came to
resemble a considerably fined-down AW.XV Atalanta,

The Albatros was an all-wood
aircraft which used a skin of
laminated plywood and balsa.
The seven aircraft were not only
some of the most beautiful civil
airliners designed in the late
1930s, but had many novel
design features

though with a retractable undercarriage, which had to
have mainwheel legs of inordinate length to stretch from
the inner engine nacelles (into which they retracted) to the
hubs of the 75-in (1.905-m) mainwheels. The Ensign was a
particularly handsome aircraft, and was planned in two
versions: European with seating for 40 passengers, and
Eastern with seating for 27 passengers. Power was provided by four 800-hp (597-kW) Armstrong Siddeley Tiger
IX radials. But progress with the type was slow, as a result
of the company's commitment to the production of the
Whitley bomber, and also to a constant stream of changes
dictated by Imperial Airways. The first aircraft finally flew
on 24 January, 1938, and the type entered service in
October of the same year. Considerable problems of
varying natures were encountered, and the Ensign was not
particularly successful until pressed into military service
after the outbreak of World War II. Fourteen examples
were built, and the main performance parameters of the
Ensign Mark II (Mark I re-engined with 950-hp [709-kW]
Wright Cyclones) included a maximum speed of 208 mph
(338 km/h) a cruising speed of 180 mph (290 km/h) and a
range of 1370 miles (2205 km).

Whereas the lines of the AW.27 can best be described as
elegant, those of DH91 Albatros can only be described as
beautiful, embodying all de Havilland's long expertise and
flair in the construction of high performance civil aircraft
of basically wooden construction. The origins of the DH91
lay in the 1934 MacPherson Robertson race to Australia,
won in fine style by the DH88 Comet. But second to this
out-and-out racer, and by an inconsiderable margin, was a
standard Douglas DC-2 airliner of KLM. So even had
European designers not earlier had food for thought about
the performance of the latest US transport aircraft, the
'MacRobertson' race's result now provided them with it. De
Havilland accordingly sought government assistance in the
development of a high-performance airliner with four

relatively small engines, superior in all important respects
to the DC-2. As usual in such discussions, progress was
slow, and it was not until the beginning of 1936 that the Air
Ministry ordered two transatlantic mailplanes (de Havilland's original concept was for a passenger aircraft) capable of carrying 1000 lb (454 kg) of mail over a range of
2500 miles (4023 km) at 210 mph (338 km/h) against a 40-
mph (64-km/h) headwind.

The first DH91 took to the air on 20 May, 1937.
Designed by A E Hagg, the Albatros was of wooden
construction, the finely tapered fuselage consisting of a
monocoque with a core of balsa sandwiched between two
layers of cedar ply, and the one-piece wing of a large
spruce box spar with wooden ribs and plywood skinning.
Very slim nacelles held the four 525-hp (392-kW) de
Havilland Gipsy Twelve inline engines in front of the
leading edges. The vertical tail surfaces were originally
twin units of typical de Havilland shape located above the
tailplane and braced by struts, but this was soon modified
to provide endplate cantilever mounting for the twin fins
and rudders. In addition to the two mailplanes, which were
handed over to the airline, Imperial Airways had ordered
five DH91s as passenger aircraft, with seating for 22
people. In service from Christmas 1938, the DH91 soon
proved itself an excellent if limited aircraft, but its activities
were soon cut short by the start of World War II.
Maximum speed was 225 mph (362 km/h), cruising speed
210 mph (338 km/h) and range 1040 miles (1674 km) as an
airliner, though range as a mailplane was 3300 miles (5310
km) with a small reduction in speeds.

The outbreak of World War II effectively halted the
further development of European civil aircraft until the
closing stages of the war. And in the USA the dominance
of the DC-3, combined with poor export chances, sufficed
to curtail the development of the latest types as purely civil
machines.

The heyday

The effect of World War II on civil aviation in Europe was inevitably to halt all but the most essential services, and these were soon being run by converted military types where there was a chance of interception by fighters. In the USA commercial operations continued, thereby strengthening the already powerful US civil market, but as in Europe design work on new aircraft continued at only a low priority until the outcome of events was quite certain. But though World War II caused a relative stagnation in civil aviation during the war, the long-term effects were highly beneficial in the technical sphere. Air transport came of age during the war, and the need to move men and equipment considerable distances and with great speed led to the rapid development of heavy transport aircraft, plus the techniques and facilities to make the optimum use of them. At public expense, therefore, designers were able to build up their knowledge of the latest aerodynamic and structural concepts, while engines improved rapidly in power, reliability and fuel economy, instrumentation developed in scope and accuracy, weather forecasting became more of a science, 'airport' facilities were built up, air- and ground-crew were trained, and the public became used to the concept of mass transportation by air. All these factors helped commercial aviation to boom soon after the war's end.

The USA, as the main supplier of transport aircraft to the Allied air forces in World War II, was thus well placed to resume its place at the head of the commercial air league: large, even vast numbers of war-surplus aircraft flooded the civil market, and soon the sky was filled with ex-military types, the most common being the C-47 and similar types (derived from the prewar DC-3) and the C-46.

But while the war had served generally to strengthen the market in short- and medium-haul airliners, it had really created the market for long-haul airliners, and here the US had total domination, with several types ready for conversion into civil machines. Thus while the UK struggled with the design and construction of types such as the mighty Bristol Brabazon (a beautifully streamlined monoplane

A British European Airways Vickers Viking 1 in the 1950s

51

BOEING 377 STRATOCRUISER

Type: four-engined long-range transport
Powerplant: four 3500-hp Pratt & Whitney Wasp Major R-4360-TSB-6 radials
Accommodation: five crew and 55 to 100 passengers
Dimensions: span 141 ft 3 in (42.9 m); length 110 ft 4 in (33.5 m)
Weights: empty 83 500 lb (37 874 kg); loaded 145 800 lb (66 133.4 kg)
Performance: maximum speed 375 mph (603 km/h); cruising speed 340 mph (547 km/h); range 4600 miles (7403 km)

with a crew of 12, seating for 100 passengers, and in its Mark 1 form powered by eight 2500-hp/1865-kW Bristol Centaurus XX radials driving four contrarotating propeller units to provide a maximum speed of 300 mph [483 km/h], a cruising speed of 250 mph [402 km/h], at 25 000 ft [7620 m], and a range of 5500 miles [8851 km]), the US were introducing their first postwar civil aircraft. The three most important of these were the Boeing 377 Stratocruiser, the Douglas DC-4 and the Lockheed L.049 Constellation.

The Boeing Stratocruiser stemmed directly from the B-29 Superfortress heavy bomber of World War II, but was in fact the civil counterpart of the KC-97 tanker/transport produced to support the B-29 and B-50 heavy bombers with air-to-air refuelling capability. Using basically the same wings, tail and engines as the two heavy bombers, the Stratocruiser presented a superficially bulbous appearance as a result of its 'double-bubble' pressurized fuselage: the upper lobe contained the passenger accommodation for 60 passengers and the flight deck, while the lower lobe contained the baggage and freight compartments, plus the

highly publicized and very popular cocktail bar and lounge. Power was provided by four 3500-hp (2611-kW) Pratt & Whitney R-4360-86 radials, giving the Stratocruiser a maximum speed of 375 mph (603 km/h), a cruising speed of 340 mph (547 km/h) at 25 000 ft (7620 m), and a range of 4600 miles (7403 km). Apart from the high cruising speed, the most notable factor here is the cruising altitude compared with that of prewar types, the ability of postwar types to cruise at altitudes well above 16 000 ft (4877 m) removing them from the low- and medium-altitude air conditions that so often proved troublesome to the passengers. Production of the Boeing 377 was limited, at only 56 examples, but the effect of these aircraft on long-haul operations, especially those across the Atlantic, were enormous. The Stratocruiser was first ordered on 28 November, 1945, when Pan American signed for 20 examples, followed on 1 April, 1946 by an American Overseas Airlines' order for eight. The type entered service with Pan American on 1 April, 1949, and flew its first transatlantic service, between New York and London, on 2 June, 1949. Such was the impact of the type

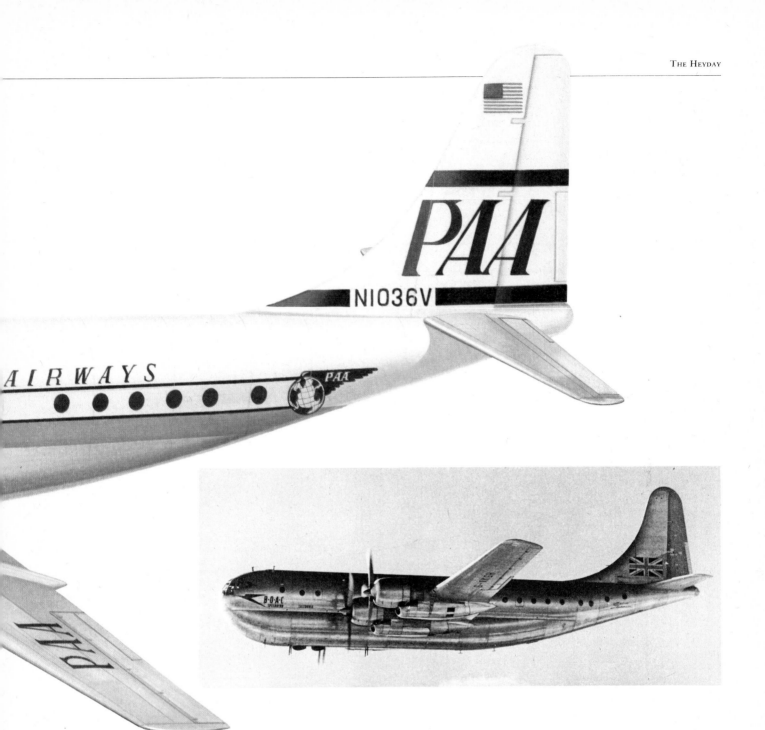

on the North Atlantic that even the British flag-carrier, British Overseas Airways Corporation, was forced to buy the type. Interestingly, the Boeing 377's operating economics were slightly worse than those of the rival DC-4 and Constellation, but this was balanced by the Boeing airliner's greater popularity as a result of the extra facilities represented by the cocktail bar and lounge.

The Douglas DC-4 beat the Boeing 377 into service by a considerable margin, the type entering service with American Airlines on 7 March, 1946. This classic aircraft owed its origins to the unsuccessful DC-4E (the E for Experimental was added to the original designation after Douglas had decided to develop the later, successful DC-4) of the late 1930s. When it became clear that the DC-4E would not meet the sponsoring airlines' requirements, the decision was made to produce a smaller and less complex pressurized airliner of low-wing, four-engined configuration, and this received the designation DC-4. Initial interest in the new type was showed by American, Eastern and United airlines of the US 'big four' domestic operators, and Pan American of the US international operators: on 26

January, 1940 these four signed contracts for 61 of the new aircraft, whose design had already begun under the leadership of A E Raymond and E F Burton. The new aircraft was about 25% lighter than the DC-4E, and smaller in all principal dimensions. Nevertheless there was a strong family resemblance, despite the replacement of the DC-4E's triple vertical tail surfaces by a single unit. Poor progress was made with the building of the first example because of the commitment of Douglas to the swelling numbers of its military aircraft, particularly from Europe. After consideration of the 1000-hp (746-kW) Wright SGR-1820-G205A Cyclone and 1050-hp (783-kW) Pratt & Whitney Twin Wasp S1C3-G radials as the basic power-plant, Douglas finally decided to install the 1450-hp (1082-kW) Pratt & Whitney R-2000 Twin Wasp 2SD1-G, and the order book began to swell satisfactorily. But with the world situation deteriorating, the US armed forces were being built up rapidly, and there was considerable demand for heavy transport aircraft. After some squabbling, the airlines and Douglas cancelled their DC-4 contracts (the first aircraft having been due for delivery at the beginning of

A Lockheed L-749 Constellation
of Eastern Airlines in flight. The
Constellation proved a long-
serving and versatile aircraft
which still operated as a cargo and
freight carrier in the late 1970s

CURTISS WRIGHT
CYCLONE 18 GR-3350

This 18-cylinder double-row geared and supercharged radial engine was used in the B-29 bomber and Martin Mars during World War II. After the war it became the powerplant for the successful Lockheed Constellation airliners.
Bore: 6.125 in (155.6 mm)
Stroke: 6.312 in (160.2 mm)
Capacity: 3347 cu in (54 847 cu cm)

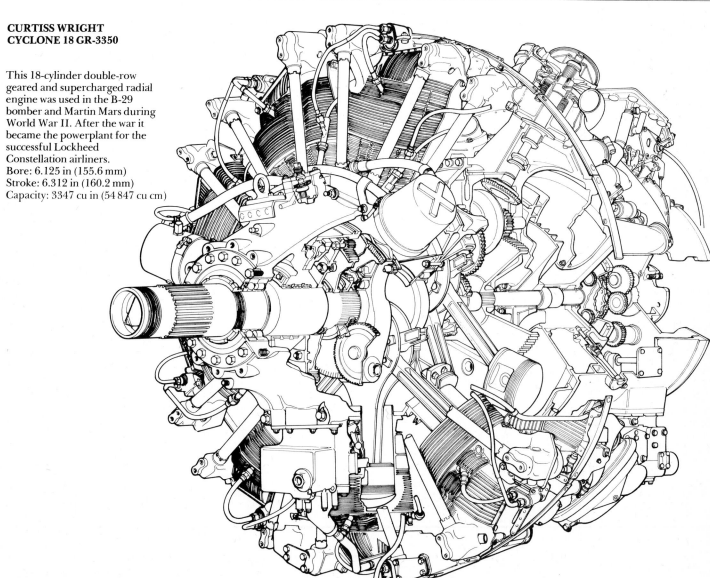

LOCKHEED SUPER CONSTELLATION L-1049G

Type: four-engined long-range transport
Powerplant: four Curtiss Wright R-3350-DA3 3250-hp radials
Accommodation: five crew and 95 passengers
Dimensions: span 123 ft (37.5 m); length 113 ft 7 in (34.5 m)
Weights: loaded 137 500 lb (62 368.6 kg)
Performance: cruising speed at 22 600 ft (6888.4 m) 355 mph (571 km/h); range 5840 miles (9398 km)

The Super Constellation was one of the postwar types which reopened routes around the world and made travellers air conscious

Above: A Lockheed L.1649 Starliner built for Trans World Airlines. It was powered by four Wright R-3350s and carried 81 passengers

Above: A Douglas DC-6 prototype; the type proved popular and efficient and is still in widespread use with charter operators

1941), and the type was instead ordered for military service as the C-54 Skymaster. The first such aircraft flew on 14 February, 1942. The airlines hoped vainly that some of the type would be released for commercial service in 1943, but the only airline use of the type was in fact restricted to contract work for the armed forces. In the event some 1163 C-54/R5D air force and navy transports were built, making the DC-4 the most widely used heavy transport of World War II. With the war's end definitely in sight, United Air Lines re-ordered 15 DC-4s on 11 September, 1944, but the order was cancelled on 24 October, 1945 when the US government began to rid itself of large numbers of surplus C-54s. At the beginning of 1946, therefore, there was a rash of C-54 airline entries, the first being Western Airlines on 18 January. Thereafter the DC-4 quickly built up a civil reputation as glowing as its military record, production of the type finally ending in August 1947 after some 2300 had been built. Immensely useful in the period immediately after the war for its availability, reliability and good payload, the DC-4 soon faded from the ranks of major passenger airliners, as a result largely of its prewar provenance, and then its take-over by the military: this meant that the type was basically too spartan for postwar operations, the more so as it was not pressurized and so limited in civilian operating altitude. But even with its disappearance from 'front-line' airline service, the DC-4 still had a great role to play in the development of civil freighting operations, which were more suited to the type's capabilities thanks to the military requirement for large loading doors, strong floors and other freighting requirements. Flight crew of the passenger version was usually four, and up to 44 passengers could be carried (high-density seating for 86 was also possible). The performance of the C-54D may be taken as typical, and included a maximum speed of 275 mph (442 km/h), a cruising speed of 203 mph (327 km/h) at 10 000 ft (3050 m), and a range of 3100 miles (4990 km/h) with a payload of 14 100 lb (6350 kg) on the power of four 1350-hp (1007-kW) Pratt & Whitney R-2000-11 radials.

The third US airliner to appear in the immediate postwar period was the great Lockheed Constellation. Whereas the keynote of the Boeing 377's success may be seen as the advanced nature of its passenger facilities and that of the DC-4 as the type's ready availability, the success of the Constellation lay in the aircraft's superb lines, which bestowed high speed and good fuel economy. As with the DC-4, the origins of the Constellation lay in the period before the USA's involvement in World War II: at the time that its main competitors were pinning their hopes on the unpressurized DC-4, TWA, under the dynamic and far-sighted control of Howard Hughes, was looking further into the aeronautical future, and decided that Lockheed would be the right company to produce the advanced, pressurized, four-engined aircraft the airline foresaw for transcontinental operations. An important aspect of TWA's requirement was that the new aircraft should have a greater pressurization differential than the Boeing 307 Stratoliner, to allow the aircraft to cruise at a considerably higher altitude.

Designed under the supervision of C L 'Kelly' Johnson, the L.049 Constellation made its first flight on 9 January,

1943. Early flight tests revealed a top speed of 347 mph (558 km/h), which was about the cruising speed of contemporary fighters and somewhat faster than the maximum speed of four-engined bombers of the period. TWA had originally contracted for 40 Constellations, but the exigencies of the wartime situation meant that the order was cancelled in favour of the military, with whom the Constellation entered service in April 1944 as the C-69 (USAAF) and R7O (US Navy). The Constellation entered full military service only in April 1945. But with victory well within sight in 1945 the US military cut their orders from 260 to 73 aircraft, and by the end of the war only 22 aircraft had been delivered. For a moment the future of Lockheed appeared bleak, but then TWA re-expressed interest in the civil Constellation, and Lockheed was able to develop a civil version of the C-69 with some speed, enabling TWA to inaugurate its transcontinental service between New York and Los Angeles on 1 March, 1946, the same day that United Air Lines started its service between New York and San Francisco with DC-4 aircraft. The two comparable routes provided a clear indication of the Constellation's superiority: quite apart from the greater comfort afforded by the pressurized Lockheed aircraft, TWA's service took only 11 hr, compared with 13 or 14 hr for the United service. TWA was unable fully to capitalize on its advantage, however, for the Constellations were grounded between 12 July and 20 September, 1946 after accidents in the cabin pressurization system resulting from supercharger failure.

The L.049 Constellation was followed by the L.649, which first flew in October, 1946, and entered service in May, 1947. Basically similar to the L.049, the L.649 was powered by 2500-hp (1865-kW) Wright R-3350-BD1 radials compared with the 2200-hp (1641-kW) R-3350-C18s of the L.049, and had more fuel tankage. Only 14 of the L.649s were ordered, supplementing the 88 L.049s. The boom in long-range passenger operations really began in 1947, and Lockheed were ready with the L.749, derived from the L.649 but having extra fuel tankage in the outer wing panels and a stronger undercarriage to cater for the increased weights possible. Some 44 were built, able to carry 55 passengers at a cruising speed of 298 mph (480 km/h) over a range of 3660 miles (5890 km), making possible intercontinental routes such as those between New York and London, and New York to Paris. The L.749A featured a further strengthened undercarriage for greater take-off weight, and 74 of this model were built.

There followed the prolific L.1049 Super Constellation series, produced in response to the development of advanced Douglas airliners with pressurized accommodation for large numbers of passengers. The L.1049 featured a fuselage stretched by 18 ft 4 in (5.59 m) and powered by four 2800-hp (2089-kW) Wright R-3350-CA1 radials, giving the type a passenger capacity of up to 95 (some 40% more than in the L.749) and a considerably lower operating cost per seat-mile at a cruising speed of 320 mph (515 km/h). The type entered service with Eastern Air Lines on 15 December, 1951, and production of the model reached 24 examples. The L.1049B was ordered for the US Air Force as the C-121 and for the US Navy as the R7V. The L.1049C was an intercontinental model which entered

service with KLM on the New York to Amsterdam route in August, 1953: powered by 3250-hp (2425-kW) Wright R-3350-DA1 Turbo-Cyclone engines, the L.1049C cruised at 330 mph (531 km/h). Some 60 of the type were built. The L.1049D was basically a freight version of the L.1049 series, capable of carrying a payload of 36000 lb (16330 kg). The L.1049E was an interim model replaced on the production line by the L.1049G, and the L.1049F was a military model procured for the USAF under designation C-121C and C-121G. The L.1049G was basically the L.1049C with improved Wright R-3350-DA3 Turbo-Cyclone engines, intended for very long-haul operations with up to 95 passengers. Cruising at 355 mph (571 km/h) at 22600 ft (6889 m), the L.1049G had a range of 5840 miles (9398 km), and 99 were built. The L.1049H, of which 53 were built, was a convertible version of the L.1049G capable of carrying 94 passengers or 44800 lb (20321 kg) of freight. The four L.1249As were experimental turbo-prop-powered models for the USAF and US Navy. The final production model of the Constellation was the L.1649A Super Constellation Starliner, of which 43 were built: powered by four 3400-hp (2536-kW) Wright R-3350-EA-2 Turbo-Cyclone engines, the Starliner featured wings increased in span from 123 ft 5 in (37.62 m) to 150 ft (45.72 m), but of thinner section than those of its predecessors, and increased fuel capacity. With up to 92 passengers, the L.1649A cruised at 342 mph (550 km/h) at 22600 ft (6889 m) and had a range of 6320 miles (10171 km) with reserves. TWA introduced the type into service on 1 June, 1957, and this was the last version of this magnificent and versatile family to enter commercial service. The location of the engines 5 ft (1.52 m) further out along the wings, and 900 lb (408 kg) of extra insulation in the fuselage helped to make the L.1649A the most popular of the series with passengers, and one of the quietest airliners.

Realizing that, in the Constellation, Lockheed had produced an airliner markedly superior to their DC-4, Douglas in 1944 decided to press ahead with the design of a pressurized model of the DC-4, to be designated DC-6. The Douglas effort was rewarded on 11 September, 1944 when the original order for 61 DC-4s placed by American, Eastern and United airlines (later cancelled in favour of military production of the C-54) was replaced with an order for 61 DC-6s. With development of a civil type at the time out of the question, the DC-6 began life as a military project for a pressurized C-54, designated XC-112, with a longer fuselage, full pressurization and more powerful 2100-hp (1567-kW) Pratt & Whitney R-2800-34 radials, ensuring much improved performance in all respects compared with the C-54. Progress was smooth, and the XC-112A first flew on 15 February, 1946.

The prospect of military sales were poor in the immediate aftermath of World War II, and Douglas devoted most of its thoughts to the development of the civil DC-6, the first of 50 ordered by American Airlines flying on 29 June, 1946. The original DC-6, of which 175 were built between 1946 and 1951, was powered by 2100-hp (1567-kW) Pratt & Whitney R-2800-CA15 radials, and could carry up to 86 passengers at 328 mph (528 km/h) over a typical range of 3340 miles (5375 km). The DC-6 was followed by the DC-6A of 1948, a cargo model

DOUGLAS DC-7C

Type: four-engined long-range transport
Powerplant: four Wright R-3350-18EA-4 Turbo-Compound piston engines
Accommodation: three crew and 105 passengers

Dimensions: span 127 ft 6 in (38.86 m); length 112 ft 3 in (34.21 m)
Weights: loaded 143 000 lb (64 860 kg); payload 21 500 lb (9750 kg)
Performance: cruising speed at 20 000 ft (6100 m) 310 mph (499 km/h); range with 15 000 lb (6800 kg) payload 4100 miles (6595 km)

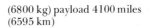

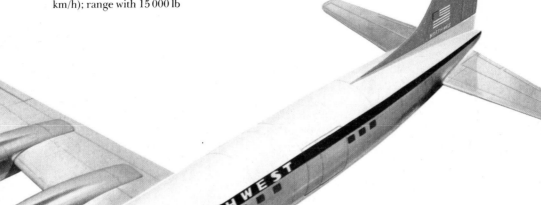

Left: A Douglas DC-7B of Eastern Airlines, 'The Great Silver Fleet'. The DC-7 could carry a crew of three to five with up to 105 passengers
Below left: A DC-7C in service with Alitalia between 1957 and 1965

Below: The Vickers Viking which was the mainstay of British commercial air operations for 18 years. It was a robust trouble-free aircraft which rarely made the headlines

Right: A view of a partially completed Airspeed Ambassador during trials in July 1947. Known as the Elizabethan Class the aircraft bore the names of Elizabethan heroes
Below: The flagship of the Elizabethan Class, G-ALZN

powered by four 2400-hp (1790-kW) Pratt & Whitney R-2800-CB16 Double Wasp radials and featuring a fuselage stretched by 5 ft (1.52 m) and greater fuel capacity. Characterized by a fuselage without cabin windows, the DC-6A could carry 28 188 lb (12 786 kg) of freight. Some DC-6As, it should be noted, were converted for passenger use by the removal of the plugs over the window spaces, and the installation of passenger equipment. The DC-6C was the production version of this type, now called convertible. Despite the increase in power, the extra payload and drag of the DC-6A and DC-6C reduced cruising speed to 315 mph (507 km/h) and maximum payload range to 2925 miles (4710 km). The DC-6B was the passenger version of the DC-6A, with 2400-hp (1790-kW) R-2800-CB16 Double Wasps or 2500-hp (1865-kW) R-2800-CB17 Double Wasps and able to carry up to 102 passengers. Like the Constellation, the DC-6 series had the useful feature of fully-reversing propellers to reduce landing run, and this feature on the DC-6A enabled the type to operate to airports with relatively short runways as part of the growing tourist business. With a maximum payload of 24 565 lb (11 142 kg), the DC-6A had a cruising speed of 315 mph (507 km/h) and a maximum payload range of 3005 miles (4835 km), though a range of 3560 miles (5730 km) was possible at a cruising speed of 280 mph (451 km/h). Production reached 287, and, unlike its main competitor the Constellation, the type was still in fairly widespread service in the late 1970s. This is largely the result of the DC-6's suitability to cargo operations when turbojet-powered airliners replaced it first on the main routes in the late 1950s and then on secondary routes in the 1960s.

The DC-7 evolved naturally from the DC-6 to use the increased power available from the 3250-hp (2425-kW) Wright R-3350 Turbo-Compound engine, in which exhaust gases from the cylinders drive a turbine coupled to the crankshaft; the extra power thus made available may be seen from the fact that the basic R-3350 developed 2500 hp (1865 kW), the extra 750 hp (560 kW) of the Turbo-Compound (otherwise called the Turbo-Cyclone) coming from the exhaust-driven turbine. The DC-7 resulted from American Airlines' conviction in 1951 that the DC-6 family could be given a new lease of life with the Turbo-Compound engine. So the original DC-7, of which 105 were built, was basically the DC-6B with the fuselage lengthened by 40 in (1.02 m) and powered by R-3350-18DA-2 Turbo-Compound engines driving four-blade propellers. American Airlines ordered 25 of the new type, which entered service on 29 November, 1953. In all, 338 of the basic family were to be produced, but the type never built up the popularity of other contemporary aircraft, as by the time of its introduction the DC-7 was approaching the end of the useful design potential of the DC-4 configuration still adhered to. The DC-6 was intended for transcontinental services, and with 99 passengers had a cruising speed of 359 mph (578 km/h) and a maximum payload range of 2850 miles (4585 km) with a payload of 20 000 lb (9072 kg).

From the DC-7 there emerged the DC-7B intercontinental model, with 3350-hp (2499-kW) R-3350-18DA4 Turbo-Compound engines. This model was externally identical with its predecessor except for longer engine nacelles, but featured increased fuel capacity. With 99 passengers the DC-7B cruised at 360 mph (579 km/h), and with a payload of 21 516 lb (9759 kg) had a maximum range of 3280 miles (5280 km). The DC-7B first flew in October 1954, and entered service on Pan American's New York to London route on 13 June, 1955.

The final version of this prolific Douglas family was the DC-7C, developed to meet a Pan American requirement for an aircraft able to operate transatlantic routes even against strong headwinds. Named the Seven Seas, the DC-7C fully met this requirement, and was in fact the world's first truly intercontinental airliner, being able to fly trans-atlantic services against even the strongest headwinds. The main difference between the DC-7C and its predecessors was the increase in wing span by 10 ft (3.05 m) to 127 ft 6 in

Below: An Avro York at
Staverton in wartime camouflage.
The York was designed and built
in six months as a military
transport in 1942. It made use of
several major Lancaster parts like
the engines and tailplane, though
a third fin was later added

Below: The York in peacetime
service. It could carry either 12
passengers and freight or 24
passengers or in the London-
South Africa run 12 passengers
with sleeping berths. Yorks were
in service for 12 years after the
war as RAF transports and civil
airliners

(38.86 m) resulting from the insertion of extra sections in the wings inboard of the inner engines, to accommodate extra fuel tankage and move the engines further from the fuselage, which was increased in length by 42 in (1.1 m) to 112 ft 3 in (34.21 m) compared with the DC-7's 93 ft 10 in (28.6 m). Apart from adding to fuel capacity, the move of the engines reduced fuselage noise, a factor much appreciated by passengers, for whom seating was increased to 105. The engines were 3400-hp (2536-kW) R-3350-18EA1 Turbo-Compounds, giving the DC-7C a cruising speed of 355 mph (571 km/h) and a range of 4605 miles (7410 km) with a payload of 23 350 lb (10 591 kg). The DC-7C first flew on 20 December, 1955, and entered service with Pan American on 1 June, 1956. Some 121 DC-7Cs were built, but the type enjoyed only a short passenger career thanks to the introduction of the first turbojet-powered aircraft on trunk routes in the late 1950s. At this time many DC-7Cs were converted into DC-7F freighters with strengthened floors and no provision for passenger operations, or sold to small airlines.

In the period immediately after World War II the British failed to compete effectively with the US in the long-range airliner market for two main reasons: very little effort had been possible towards the development of four-engined civil types during the war, allowing the US to build up a considerable head-start with the Boeing 377, the Douglas DC-4 and DC-6, and the Lockheed Constellation; and even such efforts as had been made were hampered by lack of resources, and the erroneous belief that the type with which the final British airliner would have to compete would be the unpressurized DC-4.

So while more advanced aircraft were under preparation, the British had at first to make do with converted wartime aircraft, such as the Avro Lancastrian conversion of the Lancaster bomber (four 1620-hp [1209-kW] Rolls-Royce Merlin 24 inlines, cruising speed 230 mph [370 km/h]) and the Avro York derivative of the Lancaster, first delivered in 1942 (four 1620-hp [1209-kW] Rolls-Royce Merlin 24 inlines, cruising speed 203 mph [327 km/h]). Great things were afoot, it was hoped, with the huge Bristol Brabazon, but the project was ill-conceived and technologically beyond the country in the immediate postwar period, so the first true four-engined airliner of postwar British design to enter service was the Handley Page Hermes, derived from the Hastings military transport. The decision to build a civil version of the Hastings, with a longer

fuselage, was taken in February 1945, and the initial HP68 Hermes I made its maiden flight on 3 December, 1945, crashing during the course of it. Various other schemes were tried, but the definitive model became the HP81 Hermes IV, of which 25 were built. Powered by four 2100-hp (1567-kW) Bristol Hercules 763 radials, the Hermes IV entered service in 1948 as a long- and medium-range airliner, capable of carrying up to 82 passengers at a cruising speed of 261 mph (420 km/h) over a range of 2000 miles (3219 km).

In this period immediately after World War II, most countries gave serious thought to the replacement of the DC-3 for short- and medium-haul operations. But though several countries produced aircraft intended to replace the ubiquitous DC-3, the best any of the newer aircraft did was to supplement the elderly US aircraft, available in vast numbers from war surplus stocks. The two main British contenders in this field were the beautiful Airspeed AS.57 Ambassador and the somewhat plainer Vickers Viking. Airspeed had enjoyed a limited success in civil aircraft with types such as the AS.5 Courier of 1933 and AS.6 Envoy of 1934, but the company's greatest civil type was undoubtedly the elegant AS.57 Ambassador of 1947. Although only 23 of the type were built, the Ambassador will long be remembered for its performance and looks. Introduced in prototype form in 1947, the Ambassador had a protracted development leading to too late a service entry: with 47 passengers, the high-wing Ambassador was capable of cruising at 300 mph (483 km/h) at 20 000 ft (6096 m) for a range of 720 miles (1159 km) on the power of two 2625-hp (1958-kW) Bristol Centaurus 661 radials.

The Vickers Viking was a less ambitious aircraft, but had the distinction of being Britain's first postwar commercial aircraft, and of reaching the production total of 163 examples. In its Type 610 Mark IB form, the Viking was powered by a pair of 1690-hp (1261-kW) Bristol Hercules 634 radials, and could carry up to 27 passengers at a maximum speed of 263 mph (423 km/h), and at a cruising speed of 210 mph (338 km/h) over a range of 1700 miles (2736 km).

On a smaller scale, however, two useful and interesting aircraft were produced by the British aircraft industry soon after the end of World War II: the de Havilland DH104 Dove and the DH114 Heron. The Dove was intended as an 11-seat short-range airliner, and first flew on 25 September, 1945. Powered by a pair of de Havilland

DOUGLAS DC-4

Type: four-engined medium-range transport
Powerplant: four Pratt & Whitney R-2000-2SD-13G piston engines
Accommodation: five crew and 86 passengers

Dimensions: span 117 ft 6 in (35.81 m); length 93 ft 11 in (28.63 m)
Weights: loaded 73 000 lb (33 112 kg); payload 21 373 lb (9695 kg)

Performance: cruising speed at 10 000 ft (3050 m) 204 mph (328 km/h); range with 5500 lb (2495 kg) payload 2140 miles (3440 km)

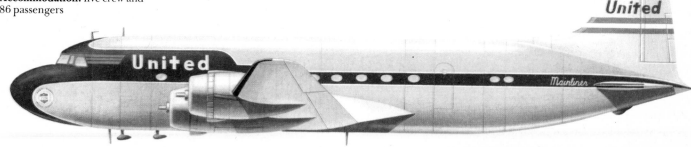

Above left: A Breguet Br 763 Provence in Air France service. The Provence could carry 107 passengers over 2291 miles (3687 km)
Left: A Vickers Viscount of Turkish Airlines. The Viscount was one of the pioneer turboprop airliners

Above: A Convair 340 medium-range airliner. It first flew in 1951 and a total of 209 were built before the introduction of the 440 Metropolitan in the mid 1950s

Gipsy Queen inline engines of between 330 and 400 hp (246 and 298 kW), the Dove could cruise at 210 mph (338 km/h) over a range of 1070 miles (1722 km) in its Dove 5 and 6 forms, and production of the series ran to over 500 examples. The Heron, introduced in 1950, was basically a four-engined version of the Dove with seating for 14 passengers. Powered by four 250-hp (187-kW) de Havilland Gipsy Queen 30 Mark 2 inlines, the Heron 2B cruised at 165 mph (266 km/h) over a range of 805 miles (1295 km). Production ran to more than 150 examples.

The US also tried to develop a successor to the DC-3, the two most successful attempts being the Convair CV-240 family, and the Martin 4-0-4. The CV-240 series evolved from the experimental CV-110, which first flew on 16 March, 1947. The type was first ordered by American Airlines, and entered service with this airline on 1 June, 1948. Able to carry 40 passengers over a range of 1800 miles (2897 km) at a cruising speed of 270 mph (435 km/h), the Convair CV-240 or Convair-Liner proved very successful and popular, especially as its comfort was considerably superior to that of any other aircraft in its class. Important innovations so far as the short- and medium-range markets were concerned were the CV-240's pressurized fuselage, tricycle undercarriage, extensive flap arrangements

and considerable economy of operation. Power was provided by two Pratt & Whitney R-2800-CA18 radials each rated at 2400 hp (1790 kW), augmented slightly by the use of exhaust ejector stubs.

The same basic engine, in its R-2800-CB16 form, the CV-340 was a natural development of the DV-240, and first entered service with United Air Lines, which had ordered 30 of the type, on 16 November, 1952, though Braniff had started a CV-340 service some 16 days earlier. Able to carry 44 passengers at a cruising speed of 284 mph (457 km/h) at 18 000 ft (5486 m) over a range of 2015 miles (3243 km), the CV-340 with its 2400-hp (1790-kW) engines was a worthy complement to the shorter-ranged CV-240. At this time the turboprop was beginning to make an impact at this level of the airline market, in the form of the Vickers Viscount, but Convair were able to develop one final piston-engined aircraft able to compete financially with the new type of aircraft. This was the CV-440 Metropolitan, which entered service with Continental Airlines on 1 April, 1956. Powered by two 2500-hp (1865-kW) R-2800-CB17 radials, the CV-440 could carry up to 52 passengers at a cruising speed of 289 mph (465 km/h) over a range equivalent to that of the two earlier models. Just as important as additional passenger capacity was the extra

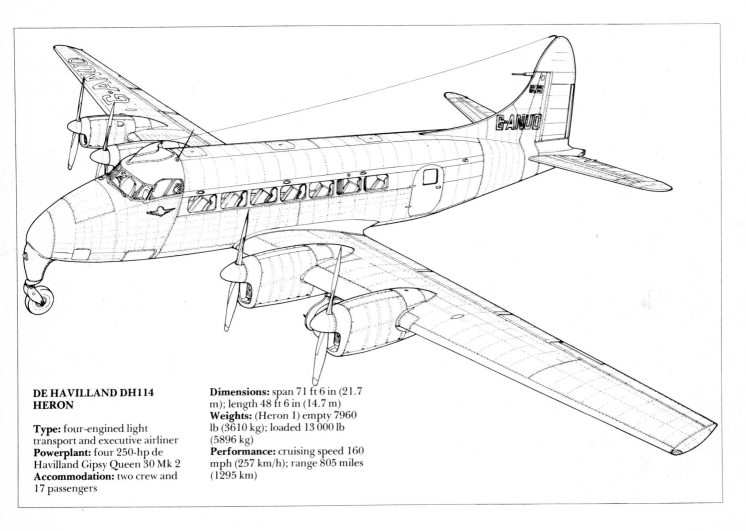

**DE HAVILLAND DH114
HERON**

Type: four-engined light
transport and executive airliner
Powerplant: four 250-hp de
Havilland Gipsy Queen 30 Mk 2
Accommodation: two crew and
17 passengers

Dimensions: span 71 ft 6 in (21.7
m); length 48 ft 6 in (14.7 m)
Weights: (Heron 1) empty 7960
lb (3610 kg); loaded 13 000 lb
(5896 kg)
Performance: cruising speed 160
mph (257 km/h); range 805 miles
(1295 km)

soundproofing incorporated, which allowed the CV-440 to
compete in passenger popularity with the inherently
quieter turboprops coming into service. Production of the
CV-240, CV-340 and CV-440 was 176, 209 and 153
respectively, and the family has since been improved by the
introduction of turboprop powerplants on these models.

The Martin 4-0-4, of which 101 commercial examples
were built, was derived from the unsuccessful Martin 2-0-2
of 1946, the first postwar US twin-engined airliner. Alterations to make the Model 4-0-4 included a fuselage
stretched by 39 in (99.06 cm), greater fuel capacity and
other improvements. The Model 2-0-2 had seemed well on
the way to success after its first flight on 22 November,
1946, just before that of the rival CV-240, and its service
entry with Northwest Airlines on 15 November, 1947. In
1948, however, a crash revealed a serious deficiency in the
wing structure, and production ended after the delivery of
the 43rd aircraft, a Model 2-0-2A with 2400-hp (1790-kW)
R-2800-CA16 radials in place of the Model 2-0-2's 2100-hp
(1567-kW) R-2800-CA18 radials. The Martin 4-0-4, of
which 101 were built for commercial operators, was
powered by the R-2800-CB16, and could carry 40 passengers at a cruising speed of 280 mph (451 km/h) over
normal route lengths of 1080 miles (1738 km).

By the middle of the 1950s, turbojets had revealed their
potential for the long-range market, and turboprops
seemed to be the up and coming powerplant for short- and
medium-haul airliners, and so design effort towards piston-engined airliners gradually tapered away, at least for
the time being. It should be noted, though, that other
countries did produce piston-engined airliners, though the
dominance of the US aircraft industry in the period
between 1945 and 1955 meant that few of these were
produced in substantial numbers. Some of the more
interesting of these types were the French Breguet Br. 763
Provence four-engined mid-wing two-deck airliner, with
four 2400-hp (1790-kW) Pratt & Whitney R-2800-CA18
radials and up to 107 passengers, carried over a range of
2291 miles (3687 km) at 217 mph (349 km/h); the Soviet Il-
14 short-range airliner, capable of carrying 28 passengers
over a range of 920 miles (1480 km) at 161 mph (260 km/h)
on the power of two 1900-hp (1417-kW) Shvetsov ASh-
82T radials; the de Havilland Canada DHC-3 Otter high-
wing braced monoplane, capable of carrying 11 passengers
at 132 mph (212 km/h) over a range of 875 miles (1410 km)
on the 600 hp (448-kW) of its Pratt & Whitney R-1340-
S1H1-G radial; and a number of other light transport or
executive aircraft.

An Armstrong Whitworth Argosy of the Imperial Airways Africa-England service in the late 1920s